THE LITERATURE
OF MUSIC

Da Capo Press Music Reprint Series

GENERAL EDITOR

FREDERICK FREEDMAN

VASSAR COLLEGE

THE LITERATURE
OF MUSIC

BY JAMES E. MATTHEW

𝄞 DA CAPO PRESS • NEW YORK • 1969

A Da Capo Press Reprint Edition

This Da Capo Press edition of
The Literature of Music is an
unabridged republication of the
first edition published in London
in 1896.

Library of Congress Catalog Card Number 69-12688

Published by Da Capo Press
A Division of Plenum Publishing Corporation
227 West 17th Street
New York, N.Y. 10011

Printed in the United States of America

THE LITERATURE
OF MUSIC

BY

JAMES E. MATTHEW

AUTHOR OF "A MANUAL OF MUSICAL HISTORY"

LONDON

ELLIOT STOCK, 62, PATERNOSTER ROW

1896

PREFACE.

———

"*LES Musiciens lisent peu,*" said one whose works on Music have been, by the irony of fate, more often reprinted than those of any other writer on the subject.

If there is any truth in this proposition (and the writer is very far from adopting it), assuredly it is from no lack of books on the subject. The Literature of Music is large, and rapidly increasing. The late C. F. Becker, in a Bibliography brought down to the year 1839, *was able to give upwards of* 6,500 *titles, a number which, since that time, has of course been enormously added to. The Wagner literature alone forms a large library! Of the principal national libraries* no classified catalogues exist, so that it is impossible to estimate the number of works which they contain on any special subject. Probably the most important and best-known Musical Library is that formed by the late M. Fétis, now the property of the Belgian nation. Apart from "practical" music and general literature, the published catalogue of it contains about 4,200 titles, a number which is slightly exceeded, however, by the writer's own library of Musical Literature, the collection of which has been so great a source of delight to him.

When, therefore, his friend the Editor of the "Book Lover's Library" suggested the following work to him, the proposition was most congenial. The only hesitation he felt was a want of confidence in his own powers, and also in the possibility of treating adequately so large a subject in so small a compass. He would gladly have handled many of the topics touched on in much greater detail, and have included others which it has been necessary to omit entirely ; but he hopes

convey may be useful to those who are tempted
to embark on a delightful study, especially as,
to the best of his knowledge, no such work
exists in this or in any other language.
His main object has been to assist the inquirer
in his search for the most useful works in
the principal departments of Musical Literature, and at the same time to give some
account of such books as are of interest, either
for their curiosity, for their scarceness, or
for the important influence they may have
exercised in a past age.

NOTE.

It may be well to bear in mind, with regard to the somewhat puzzling termin-ations of the Latin word "Musica," that it is declined both in the Latin, and also in the Greek form, while in early manuscripts and printed books the genitive "æ" often takes the form of a simple "e." Thus we find the genitive written indifferently as Musicæ, Music*e, and* Musices, *while the accusative appears both as* Musicam *and* Musicen.

CONTENTS.

x   *Contents.*

LITERATURE OF MUSIC.

CHAPTER I.

The Literature of Ancient Music.

THE familiar description of Jubal in the book of Genesis as "the father of all such as handle the harp and organ" is the earliest mention in literature of the art of Music, and many other references in the Bible, chiefly in the Old Testament, will be familiar to every reader.

It will not be supposed that the translations of the names of the different instruments can be accepted as more than approximations. At the time the Authorised Version was made no adequate knowledge of the subject existed, and in many cases no exact equivalent was to be found among the instruments then in use. The difficulty of the investigation

commended it to almost every commen-
tator.   Among the most celebrated of
these we may mention the learned
Benedictine Dom Calmet, in his *Com-
mentaire littéral* (Paris, 1714-20), an
enormous work in twenty-six volumes
quarto.   Another, and an earlier writer,
of whom we shall have to speak again,
Père Marin Mersenne, possessed more
ample qualifications for the task.   He projected a commentary on the Book of Genesis
—*Quæstiones celeberrimæ in Genesim* (Paris,
1623: folio), with a view of confut-
ing certain objections to the Mosaic
Cosmogony.   The good father was a man
of universal acquirements, but the art of
Music was his delight, and the mention of
Jubal an opportunity which was irresist-
able.   It served as the text for a disquisi-
tion, not only on the music of the Hebrews,
but also of the Greeks, and even of the
Moderns.   It extends to one hundred
pages folio, with a supplement of thirty-one
pages.   With so long a commentary on a
single text, it is not surprising that the
author found himself compelled to bring
his work to a conclusion at the end of
the sixth chapter, having already occupied
one thousand one hundred and seventy-
five pages !

It cannot be said that the labours of

these, and of many other earnest workers
in the same field, threw much light on
the subject of Jewish music ; nor were the
professed historians of Music much more
fortunate.   Each of them was of course
bound to begin at the earliest times, and to
say all that he knew,—and much that he
imagined,—on the music of the Hebrews.
In truth the requisite materials were not
available, nor did it occur to any one that
the Jews in 'all probability acquired whatever knowledge of the arts they possessed
during their sojourn of three hundred
years in the land of Egypt ; nor would
this have appreciably advanced the matter,
as information about the music of Egypt
was equally wanting.

Strange to say, when the first piece of
solid information was brought to light, the
learned public received it with scorn.
The well-known traveller Bruce communicated to Dr. Burney a copy of a painting
of an Egyptian harp which he claimed to
have discovered in an ancient tomb.   It
was reproduced in the first volume of
Burney's   *History.*   The instrument ap-
proximated so nearly to the modern form
that it was believed to have existed only
in Bruce's imagination ; subsequent discoveries, however, have proved the absolute correctness of the drawing.

It is well known that when General Bonaparte made his expedition into Egypt, he organised a body of *savants* to investigate the monuments and antiquities of that country. Among these was G. A. Villoteau, a well-qualified musician. The result of his researches will be found in the magnificent work published by the French Government, *La Description de l'Eypte* (Paris, 1809-26 : 20 vols., folio) ; a second edition was published by Panckoucke in octavo, in which form it is more readily to be met with. The articles by Villoteau will be found in vols. vii., viii., xiii., xiv., and were by far the most valuable contributions to the knowledge of the subject up to that date. This was followed in 1836 by the publication of Sir J. Gardner Wilkinson's work on the Ancient Egyptians, better known in the popular edition, which has been reprinted several times, and contains much useful and trustworthy information on the subject of Music in that country.

In the meantime many specimens of Egyptian instruments found their way into museums, and still more numerous representations of them were discovered depicted on the tombs and other buildings of ancient Egypt. In 1847 the world was astonished by the discoveries of Sir A. H.

(then Mr.) Layard in the mounds of Nimrood and Kouyunjik. The sculptured slabs and other objects which he unearthed and sent to the British Museum contained many representations of the musical instruments in use by the Assyrians. These found an interpreter in the late Mr. Carl Engel, whose work, *The Music of the Most Ancient Nations* (London, 1864: 8vo) is a most able investigation of the subject, on which it must be considered the standard work. A useful and popular little book under the title of *The Music of the Bible* (London, 1879: 8vo) was written by Sir. J. Stainer, based mainly on the conclusions of Engel. It has been contended that Plain-Song is identical with the music used in the Jewish Temple. This view is advocated with much conviction and learning by the Rev. Arthur Bedford in his *Temple Musick* (London, 1706: 8vo).

It is not till the later period of Grecian history that we meet with any actual treatise on the art of Music. The tenets of Pythagoras on this and other subjects are handed down to us by tradition only, but he still lives in the literature of Music in the oft-repeated story of his discovery of the ratio of musical intervals by the different notes produced from an anvil

when struck by hammers of varying
weights. No such result is produced, as
simple experiment would have proved,
but the anecdote was universally repeated
by the old writers, and the supposed
discovery is said to have led him to
investigate the divisions of the monochord.

Passing over something more than two
centuries we come to Aristoxenus—
(probably the author of the earliest treatise
on music which has come down to us)—
Euclid, Eratosthenes, Alypius, and, extending into the Christian era, Plutarch,
Ptolemy, Nicomachus and others, forming
a considerable mass of literature. The
subject of Greek music is one of extraordinary complexity, but it may be said
that the main purpose of these treatises
is to explain the construction of the
various scales at that time in use. Manuscripts of these and of other Greek works
on Music are to be found in many of the
large libraries. The first to find its way
into print was a Latin translation, by
G. Valla, of a treatise purporting to be
by Cleonides, which was published at
Venice in 1497 in folio, forming part of a
volume containing other treatises, including that of Vitruvius on Architecture.
It turns out that the supposed work of

Cleonides is identical with a treatise attributed in several MSS. to Euclid, the famous geometrician, and the rival claims have not been settled, although it has been pointed out by the great English mathematician Wallis that the work is inconsistent with another treatise of Euclid known as *The Section of the Canon*—*i.e.*, the division of the monochord. Be this as it may, the Greek texts of both works were first published in Paris by the mathematician Pena, with a Latin translation (1557 : 4to). In 1562 Gogavinus gave an edition, but in Latin only, of the writings of Aristoxenus and Ptolemy (Venice : 4to). The work was undertaken at the instance, as he tells us in the preface, of the famous Venetian theorist Zarlino. In 1616 the eminent scholar Meursius published for the first time (Leyden, L. Elzevir : 4to) the Greek texts of Aristoxenus, Nicomachus, and Alypius, with notes.

But the greatest impetus to the study of Greek music was given by the publication by Marcus Meibomius of his *Antiquæ Musicæ Auctores Septem* (Amsterdam, L. Elzevir, 1652 : 2 vols., 4to)—a book which, in spite of certain imperfections, is indispensable to every one who wishes to study the subject. The seven authors are Aristoxenus, Euclid, Nicomachus,

Alypius, Gaudentius, Bacchius senior, and Aristides Quintilianus. To all these a Latin translation is appended, as well as numerous notes, and a Latin treatise of Martianus Capella is added.

Meibomius was a native of Schleswig-Holstein, his real name being Meybaum, which he Latinised, according to the pedantic habit of the time. He dedicated his work to Christina, Queen of Sweden, who persuaded him to take up his residence at her Court. In an evil moment he was induced to give a performance of what he conceived to be a true specimen of Greek music. Great as were his theoretical acquirements, he was unfortunately deficient both in ear and voice. His rendering so excited the risibility of the courtiers, that, losing his temper, he boxed the ears of the Queen's physician, who seems to have planned the exhibition. The result was that Meibomius had to leave the Court.

It may be mentioned that the treatise of Bacchius senior was also twice printed by Mersenne—firstly in Latin, in the place where one would be most unlikely to look for it—in his *Quæstiones celeberrimæ in Genesim*, of which we have already spoken, and secondly in French in his *Traité de l'Harmonie* (Paris, 1627 : 8vo).

The Latin treatise of Martianus Capella, who was a much later writer, living about A.D. 475, forms part of a series on the seven liberal arts, entitled *De nuptiis Philologiæ et Mercurii.* The *editio princeps* is Vicenza 1499 folio. It is this work which Grotius edited when only fifteen years of age (Leyden, 1599 : 8vo).

The publication of original texts was worthily continued by the great English mathematician Wallis, who in 1682 (Oxford : 4to) gave an excellent edition of the *Harmonicorum Libri Tres* of Claudius Ptolemæus, the celebrated geographer, together with a Latin translation and elucidations. This was reprinted in the collection of his mathematical works (Oxford, 1695-9 : 3 vols., folio), with the addition of a commentary on it by Porphyry, and also of the Harmonics of Bryennius, a very much later work (A.D. 1320), but which is valuable, as it contains many extracts from earlier writers.

The Περὶ Μουσικῆς of Philodemus was the last work to be brought to light. The author's name was mentioned by Cicero, but none of his writings were known until a manuscript was found at Herculaneum containing a portion of his work on Music. Unlike the treatises we have been speaking of, this consists of a consideration of the question whether the pursuit of the art is worthy of praise or of blame. The papyrus was unrolled with great difficulty, being much charred. Printed most luxuriously, it forms the first volume of the edition of the recovered manuscripts. It is engraved in facsimile on thirty-nine copper plates, with a letter-press reprint facing each plate in which the *lacunæ* existing in the MSS. are restored in red ink. A Latin translation is supplied, accompanied by a commentary and notes, and it forms a volume of great magnificence and interest. The title is *Herculanensium Voluminum quæ supersunt Tomus I.* (Neapoli, 1793 : folio).

It remains to mention the Dialogue of Plutarch on music, which forms the main source of information as to the *history* of the art among the Greeks. The editions are so numerous that it is unnecessary to specify any one in particular.

We have now recorded the principal works on which our knowledge of Greek music is based. Some of them are available in more modern form ; for instance, Aristoxenus has been edited, with a German translation, by Paul Marquard (Berlin, 1868 : 8vo), and there is a French translation by C. E. Ruelle (Paris, 1871 : 8vo). F. Bellermann edited the treatise of Bacchius senior (Berlin, 1841 : 4to) with a second part not found in Meibomius. An English translation of the *Canon of Euclid* will be found in Davy's *Letters addressed to a Young Gentleman* (Bury St. Edmunds, 1787 : 2 vols., 8vo), while Plutarch, *De Musica*, was edited, with a Latin translation, by R. Volkmann (Leipzig, 1856 : 8vo) and by R. Westphal (Breslau, 1865 : 8vo). An English translation of this author, beautifully printed by C. Whittingham (London, 1822 : 8vo), said to have been made by J. H. Bromby, of Hull, to present to his friends, is met with but seldom. And in 1895 Carolus Janus (Jahn?) has edited in a cheap and handy volume *Musici Scriptores Græci*, comprising Aristotle, Euclid, Nicomachus, Bacchius, Gaudentius, and Alypius, together with all the known examples of Grecian melody (Leipzig, 1895 : 8vo).

If the reader is disposed to enter the thorny path of the study of Greek music he may well bear in mind the remark of Dr. Burney that "he never understood the Greek music, nor found any one that did ! " If he still persevere, there is no lack of writers anxious to help him on the way. Passing over the works of Burette, to be found in the Mémoires of the

Académie des Inscriptions (1717-21), the *Dialogue sur la Musique des Anciens*, published anonymously, but by the Abbé de Chateauneuf (Paris, 1725 : 12mo), and the *Mémoire sur la Musique des Anciens* of the Abbé Roussier (Paris, 1770 : 4to), are both well-known works and readily obtainable. The *Theory of Harmonics* of John Keeble (London, 1784 : 4to) may also be consulted. But the student will probably find greater help from more modern writers, especially from the Germans— Drieberg, F. Bellermann, R. Westphal, and C. F. Weitzmann. The eminent French mathematician A. J. H. Vincent, in addition to editing some of the musical MSS. in the Paris libraries, with copious elucidations, wrote much on the subject ; but he had an inveterate habit of dissipating his powers in controversial pamphlets, which are of course not easy to meet with. The greatest work of all is that by F. A. Gevaert—*Histoire et Théorie de la Musique de l'Antiquité* (Ghent, 1875, 1881 : 2 vols., 8vo). It is a work of enormous research, comprising all that is known of the subject up to the present time. It is much to be regretted that so admirable a book should be issued without an index.

It may be well to mention here, that while such a mass of Greek literature on

Music has been handed down to us, until some recent discoveries three authentic fragments only of Greek music were known to exist. They were first printed by Vincenzo Galilei in his *Dialogo della Musica Antica e Moderna* (Florence, 1581 : folio). The object of the work was to exalt the music of antiquity at the expense of the music of the day. The great revival of classical studies had disposed certain minds to believe that the excellence of the ancients was paramount in all the arts alike. The opinion died hard ; in 1647—that is, sixty-six years later —the learned G. B. Doni published his treatise, *De præstantia Musicæ Veteris* (Florence : 4to), in which he advocates the same views ; and writers of even a later date shared the prejudice.

We must also mention another question which has been hotly contested—whether harmony, as we understand it, was practised by the Greeks. Even now the question cannot be considered settled. The paper read by Fétis before the Académie Royale de Belgique (vol. xxxi., April 1858) is readily obtainable and forms an excellent *résumé* of the subject, although written in opposition to the claim.

CHAPTER II.

The Mediæval Writers on Music.

T will have been remarked that, with the exception of the work of Martianus Capella, the language of all the treatises on Music which we have mentioned has been Greek. It is not till we arrive at the threshold of the Middle Ages that we find any original work on the subject in Latin. One writer then appeared whose treatise on Music acquired an unfortunate popularity—Boethius—for it is quite certain that he possessed no practical acquaintance with the subject. His work was based on those treatises of which we have been speaking in the last chapter, the purport of which he so completely misunderstood as to render darker what was already sufficiently difficult of comprehension. Partly owing to the extraordinary admiration in which his character was held, still more probably to the fact that he wrote in Latin, his treatise was accepted as the acknowledged text-book. Its approximate date is A.D. 500.

No manuscripts are more common than the works of Boethius, and very soon after the invention of printing copies were still further multiplied. The earliest edition of the *De Institutione Musica* was printed at Venice in 1492, folio, but the best of the old editions is that published at Basle in 1570, folio, in which the work on Music was edited by Glareanus, a scholar distinguished for his knowledge of that art, of whom we shall have to speak again later. The authority of Boethius made itself felt for centuries, and it is only recently that its baselessness has been exposed.

A knowledge of the science of Music was confined almost exclusively to the ecclesiastics. A certain acquaintance with it was necessary for the proper rendering of the offices of the Church, and many treatises were written, almost invariably by priests, with the object of supplying this knowledge, MSS. of which existed in most of the monastic libraries, and are now valuable as a means of tracing the gradual progress of musical art.

It is entirely owing to the labours of two eminent antiquaries that it has been possible for modern students to become acquainted with these precious remains of a remote antiquity. The first to shake the dust from these old parchments was Martin Gerbert, Prince Abbot of the Monastery of St. Blaise in the Black Forest, a man who, by his many virtues, earned the respect and affection of all the country round, and, by his publications on the art which he loved, secured the gratitude of all musical students. In 1784 he brought out his *Scriptores Ecclesiastici de Musica Sacra potissimum* in three volumes quarto, printed in the monastery. It contains about forty works, many of them of the highest interest, arranged chronologically, dating from the fourth to the fifteenth centuries. The whole ground of the development of musical notation is covered, from the time of St. Isidore of Seville (seventh century), who denied the possibility of preserving melodies otherwise than by tradition, "*quia scribi non possunt,*" to the perfected system virtually identical with that now in use. We have not space to give a complete table of the contents, but we find the *Musica enchiriadis* of Hucbald, with his ingenious notation which was so great an advance on the Neumes; several treatises by Guido d'Arezzo—the musician for whom so much has been claimed, but whose actual per-

formances it is so difficult to estimate ; it
is probably safe, however, to attribute to
him the system of hexachords, which for
so many centuries added to the difficulties
of musical study—for an explanation of
which we must refer the reader to the
article "Hexachord" in Grove's *Dictionary*
or to that on "Musical Notation" in Stainer
and Barrett's *Dictionary*—and also of the
"Guidonian Hand" a *memoria technica* of
this elaborate system. We may further
mention the *Musica* of Cotton, in which
he so clearly sets forth the imperfections
of the system of Neumes, as well as the
treatises of Franco of Cologne, Joannes
de Muris and Adam de Fulda.

It has been said that Gerbert was not
sufficiently critical in the choice of the
authors whose works he printed, and that
he did not always avail himself of the
best MSS. This may probably be true,
but it must be remembered that at that
time most of these works were lying unknown and forgotten on the shelves of
monastic libraries, which had probably
never been catalogued. One of the
results of the Napoleonic wars was the
suppression of these houses and the
absorption of the literary treasures which
they contained in public libraries, where
they became available. We may regret

these shortcomings, but must be thankful
to the good Abbot who was the first to
break ground in an unexplored country.

It is to a learned French antiquary,
Edmond de Coussemaker, that we are
indebted for a continuation of the work
so well begun by Gerbert.   Although
esteemed as a lawyer, and acting as *juge
de paix* successively in several towns in
French Flanders, he found time to produce a series of works of the greatest
value on the musical literature of the
Middle Ages.   His first work, the
Mémoire sur Hucbald, originally published
in the proceedings of the Société Royale
de Douai, was printed separately from
the same type, but in quarto and with a
new title, dated Paris, 1841.   The work
is a running commentary on the treatises
of Hucbald printed by Gerbert, and it had
the merit of being the first to bring
prominently to the notice of musicians
the importance of these treatises to the
history both of notation and of harmony.
The merit of Hucbald is that, more than
a century before Guido d'Arezzo, he contrived a system of notation, which, unlike
the Neumes then employed, gave a definite
pitch to the note, and also a graphic representation of a musical passage—in fact,
he was very near to the invention of our

existing notation. His plan consisted in using the spaces alone to represent the notes, and in writing the syllables of the words in the spaces indicating the successive notes of the melody. No notes were placed on the lines; their only function was to separate the spaces. The principal objection to this method is the room it occupies. Strange to say, it seems to have been used by the inventor only, and the ordinary music stave to have had an altogether independent development.

The work on which Coussemaker's fame will probably rest is the admirable continuation of Gerbert's *Scriptores*. This was commenced in 1864 under the title of *Scriptorum de Musica Medii Ævi novam seriem a Gerbertina alteram collegit E. de Coussemaker.* The fourth and concluding volume was brought out in 1876, shortly after the death of the compiler. The work contains about seventy treatises, mostly distinct from those in Gerbert, except in a few cases where the editor has had access to a better or more complete manuscript. Among the most interesting is a long series of the works of Tinctoris, a writer not represented at all in Gerbert. This includes his *Diffinitorium*, which was one of the earliest books on Music to receive the honour of the printing press.

This collection, however, forms but a small part of the labours of M. de Coussemaker. Not to mention lesser works, we are indebted to him for a *Histoire de l'Harmonie au Moyen Age* (Paris, 1852), and *L'Art Harmonique aux XIIe et XIIIe Siècles* (Paris 1865), both in quarto, in which this interesting subject is investigated with great skill and research ; also for his *Drames Liturgiques du Moyen Age* (Paris, 1861 : 4to), an interesting account of the precursors of the Oratorio,—and for an edition of the works of the troubadour Adam de la Halle (Paris, 1872 : large 8vo). The one thing to regret about the works of Coussemaker is their great and increasing value. They are all printed with much luxury, profusely illustrated with admirable facsimiles, and produced in limited editions, so that they have become valuable possessions.

It will be seen that the collections of Meibomius, Gerbert, and Coussemaker, contain nearly all that is valuable from the time of the Greeks to that of the invention of printing.

CHAPTER III.

Early Works on Music after the Invention of Printing.

T is remarkable how treatises on Music were multiplied almost immediately after the invention of printing. There is but little doubt that the *Diffinitorium Musices* of Tinctoris was the first musical work to see the light. This volume, a small quarto, was printed at Treviso, about the year 1474. It is a work of the greatest rarity. Dr. Burney found a copy in the library of George III., which is now in the King's Library at the British Museum, and a copy was discovered at Gotha, by Forkel, the well-known historian of Music. It is a little galling to learn that a copy in the Heber sale was knocked down for one shilling! The work has been frequently reprinted.

The earliest work with a date is the *Theoricum opus armonice discipline* of

Franchinus Gaforius, printed in Naples in 1480, quarto, and that there was already a public for works of this nature is proved by the numerous editions of this writer's works which followed in rapid succession. The titles of the works of Gaforius show that he was endowed with a good share of self-esteem, unless the apparent vanity should be attributed to his printer.   In this work, for example, the title reads, *Clarissimi et Præstantissimi Musici Franchini Gafori . . . Opus.*   A second edition was printed at Milan in 1492, folio, with some changes. The work begins with a long series of quotations from all the authors of antiquity, sacred and profane, who have spoken in praise of Music.   It then proceeds with an exposition of the principles of Music, based on the writings of Boethius, followed by an explanation of the music of the Greeks, the division of the monochord and the solmisation of Guido d'Arezzo. The many diagrams are boldly cut in wood, and there are exceedingly rough and somewhat comic cuts of the anvil of Pythagoras, and the applications of the principles he was supposed to have drawn from it to bells, musical glasses, strings, and pipes, but it contains no example of musical notation.

This work was followed by the *Practica*

Musice, the first edition of which was
printed in Milan in 1496. It was reprinted at Brescia in 1497 and 1502, and
at Venice in 1512, all in folio. It consists
mainly of instructions in Plain-Song,
measurable music, and counterpoint, and
contains a large number of musical
illustrations, all engraved on wood. The
title of the first edition, and the borders
of the opening pages of Books I. and II.
which are repeated in Books III. and IV.
show considerable skill, and are a great
advance on the illustrations to the previous
works. In the edition of 1502 all the
examples and the table of the lengths of
organ pipes are printed from the identical
blocks used in the first edition. In the
Venetian edition these have all been
re-engraved.

The third work of Gaforius was the
*De Harmonia Musicorum Instrumen-
torum Opus,* published at Milan in 1518
(folio), of which this edition alone exists.
On the title-page is a woodcut, repre-
senting the author addressing his disciples,
who are seated on the floor, while he
occupies a desk, duly supplied with an
hour-glass. The book is a learned—one
may say pedantic—treatise on the music
of the Greeks. One of its principal
points of interest consists in a short life

of the author, by Pantaleone Melegoli, which is appended to it.

These are the three original works of Gaforius, but in 1508 he published at Milan, in folio, his *Angelicum ac divinum opus musice ; materna lingua scriptum.* This was an epitome of the *Theoricum Opus*, and of the *Practica Musice*, in the Italian language, which he adopted in consequence of the imperfect scholarship of many musicians, who were unable to understand his other works.

Gaforius was also concerned in a controversy which was carried on with extraordinary bitterness. In 1482 a Spanish musician, Ramis de Pareja, settled in Bologna and founded a music-school. In that year he published a book, now of the very greatest rarity, in which he criticised with freedom the system of Guido. The point at issue was that the system of hexachords made no provision for the fact that if the fifths were in perfect tune the thirds would require to be adjusted, and *vice versâ*. It is the earliest notice of a difficulty which has continued to occupy the attention of musicians to the present time. This brought forth a vigorous rejoinder from Nicolaus Burtius (Bologna, 1487 : 4to)—*Musices Opusculum; cum defensione Guidonis Aretini adversus*

quendam hyspanum veritatis prevarica-
torem; a book which has an additional interest, as containing the earliest example
of printed music. Spartaro, a pupil of
Ramis, replied, asserting that Burtius was
incapable of understanding the subject
(Bologna, 1491 : 4to). When Gaforius
published his *De Harmonia Musicorum*
Instrumentorum in 1518 he expressed
with great decision his opposition to the
views of Ramis. It would seem that
letters must have passed between Gaforius
and Spartaro on the subject, in which the
discussion grew warmer, and it has been
suggested that Spartaro was urged on by
those who were jealous of the position
held by Gaforius. However this may
be, Gaforius, now a old man, was at last
roused to fury, which he allowed to
explode in his *Apologia adversus Johannem*
Spartarium et complices musicos Bon-
onienses (Turin, 1520: folio). In it he
becomes roundly abusive, and accuses
Spartaro of daring to teach Music when
he is grossly ignorant of it, and of Latin,
and of every other form of learning.
Spartaro lost no time in replying in his
Errori di Franchino Gafurio da Lodi :
Da Maestro Joane Spartario Musico,
Bolognese : in sua deffensione : & del suo
preceptore Maestro Bartolomeo Ramis

Hispano : Subtilimente demonstrati (Bologna, 1521 : 4to). He heads his preface *In Franchinum Gafurium Laudensem invectiva* ; and the last word accurately describes the style of the book. It is addressed throughout to Gaforius in the second person singular, and all his supposed errors are duly tabulated. No reply to this work has been found, but that one must have been made by Gaforius or his friends is proved by the fact that in May of the same year Spartaro returns to the charge with a pamphlet entitled, *Dilucide et probatissime Demonstratione de Maestro Joanne Spartario Musico Bolognese, contra certe frivole et vane excusatione Da Franchinus Gafurio* (*Maestro de li errori*) *in luce aducte.* In 1522 Gaforius died and the controversy ended, although in 1531 Spartaro brought out a *Tractato di Musica* in a great measure directed against the views of the old master.

It may be remarked that Gaforius spelt his name indifferently as Gaforius, Gafforius, and Gafurius, and that by early Italian writers he is frequently referred to as Franchinus.

Another famous writer of a rather later date was Pietro Aaron, or Aron—for he also adopted variety in spelling his name.

A priest, as was Gaforius, and a native of Florence, he is said to have published his first work, *Dell 'Istituzione armonica*, at Bologna, in 1516 ; but the publication of any work under such a title is open to considerable doubt, for it is only known by a Latin translation, made by his friend, J. A. Flaminius, which appeared in that year (Bologna : 4to). Probably Aaron was not so good a scholar as Gaforius, for all his original works are in Italian. The principles enunciated in the book just mentioned had the result of drawing him into the controversy of which we have already spoken, and he received some rough treatment from Gaforius. In all probability he was one of the *Complices Musici Bononienses* who so sadly excited the ire of Gaforius. The work by which he is best known is his *Toscanello in Musica*, which passed through five editions, all printed at Venice in folio, in the years 1523, 1525, 1529, 1539, and 1562—the last after the death of the author. He travels over the same ground as Gaforius, and was no doubt the foremost representative of the rival school of Bologna. The title is supposed to have been intended as a compliment to his native country. According to Fétis the rules of counterpoint are well explained. In the edition of 1549, and subsequently, he added a chapter on Plain-Song, but he had already in 1525 brought out a treatise on the eight tones, under the title of *Trattato della Natura et Cognitione di Tutti gli tuoni di Canto Figurato* (Venice, 1525 : folio). Both these works are furnished with a large wood engraving of the author in the act of lecturing to his pupils; and in a little book of a much more miscellaneous character, entitled *Lucidario in Musica* (Venice, 1545 : 4to) we find a portrait taken later in life, with a copy of verses headed *Virga Aron floruit.* This work discusses many opinions held by different authorities on points of musical interest, and in it we find a list of some of the principal musicians of the day, both professional and amateur, including many ladies, so that the book is of great historical interest.

The proportions of the intervals of the scale continued to engross the attention of most of the learned musicians. Among these we have Ludovicus Foglianus, whose *Musica Theorica docte simul ac dilucide pertractata* (Venice, 1529: folio) is of great interest. It is divided into three Books, the first of which treats of the proportions of intervals, the second of consonances, and the third of the division of the

monochord. The book is profusely illustrated with remarkable diagrams showing
the relative proportions of the intervals,
and also of the use of the monochord.
Some of these are reproduced in Hawkins's
notice of this author, but not in a manner
to do justice to the originals.

But the greatest of the early Italian
theorists was undoubtedly Gioseffe Zarlino
of Chioggia, Maestro di Capella at St.
Mark's in Venice—a man of great acquirements in all departments of learning,
whose love for Music led him to devote
his best energies to its advancement.
He is principally known as the author of
two treatises—*Istitutioni Armoniche,* first
printed in Venice in 1558, folio, reprinted
1562 and 1573, and *Dimostrationi Armoniche* (Venice, 1571 : folio), reprinted
1573.

The first Book of the *Istitutioni* comprises the usual dissertation in praise of
Music, its uses, and its varieties, together
with an explanation of such arithmetical
rules as are required in the consideration
of musical problems. The second Book
is devoted to the proportion of intervals ;
and in it he advocates a form of scale
known as the *Synotonous,* or *Intense
Diatonic,* of Ptolemy, which is virtually
identical with our modern major scale in

just intonation. The third Book expounds the laws of counterpoint, and the fourth treats of the Church Modes.

The *Dimostrationi* have a dramatic setting. Zarlino tells us that in 1562, in the month of April, Adrian Willaert, the famous founder of the Venetian School, was laid up with gout. During his illness his friends Claudio Merulo, Francesco Viola, Maestro di Capella to Alfonso d'Este, and Zarlino, were in the habit of cheering him by meeting at his house to converse on various topics of musical interest. The *Dimostrationi* is a report of the discussions of these " Friends in Council."

The views of Zarlino were not allowed to pass without controversy. His former pupil, Vincentio Galilei, a man of considerable learning, a good musician, and the father of the more celebrated Galileo Galilei, attacked them with much violence in his *Dialogo della Musica Antica e Moderna* (Florence, 1581 : folio), a book of great musical interest, to which we have already referred (p. 13). In 1589 Zarlino published a complete edition of his works in four volumes folio (Venice). Vol. iii. is entitled *Sopplimenti Musicali*, which, while going over much of the same ground as his previous work, is also a reply to the attack of his old pupil. It is worthy of note that while the other volumes are dated 1589, this third volume is dated 1588, having probably been published out of its turn in order to answer Galilei. The tone of the reply differs widely from the attack, and should have protected the venerable master from the intemperate rejoinder of Galilei, *Discorso intorno all' opere di messer Gioseffo Zarlino da Chioggia* (Florence, 1589 : 8vo)—a little book which possesses one curious characteristic. Although containing one hundred and thirty-four pages, from beginning to the end of the book there is no break of paragraph ; and as it is without index, to find any particular statement is almost hopeless.

Another very learned theorist of a slightly later period was Ludovico Zacconi whose *Prattica di Musica* (Venice, 1592 ; reprinted, 1596 ; with a second part, 1619 : folio), forms a complete handbook, covering the whole range of the musical knowledge of the time. The author possessed great clearness of exposition— a gift to be valued by those who are studying the abstruse musical systems of that day.

The writings of Bottrigari deserve to be mentioned, principally on account of

a curious mystification attaching to one
of them.   His first work, *Il Patricio overo
de' tetracordi di Aristossene* (Bologna,
1593 : 4to), is sufficiently described by
its title.   The book about which discussion has arisen is *Il Desiderio, overo
de' Concerti di varij Strumenti Musicali.
Dialogo di Alemanno Benelli* (Venice,
1594 : 4to).   The work was actually by
Bottrigari, but, not wishing his own name
to appear, his friend Annibal Melone
lent his, under the anagram of Alemanno
Benelli.   The title, *Il Desiderio*, is taken
from the name of one of the interlocutors
in the dialogue of which the work consists, Grazioso Desiderio, the other being
Alemanno Benelli.   It appears that subsequently Melone claimed the work as his
own, to the annoyance of Bottrigari, who,
according to Fétis, proceeded to reprint
it at Bologna in 1599 (4to), and that
Melone brought out another edition under
his own name at Milan in the year 1601,
which consists simply of the old "remainder" of 1594, with a new title.   We
have before us a copy of the 1599 edition
with the name of Bottrigaro (*sic*) on the
title.   With the exception of the title,
prefatory matter, and index, it is identical
with that of 1594, differing in this only,
that throughout the work a little slip, "*Del*

S. C. Herc. Bottrig.," has been very carefully pasted over the original heading,
" *Di Alemanno Benelli.*" The work itself
is interesting, as showing the ideas about
orchestral music in those days.

On account of its beauty we must
mention the charming little *Compendium
Musices* (Venice, Lucantonio de Giunta,
1513 : 8vo)—a little manual of Plain-Song
printed in red and black—a book several
times re-issued under the title of *Can-
torinus*.

Germany was not far behind Italy in
its production of works on Music. The
earliest known work is the *Flores Musice
omnis cantus Gregoriani*, which was
printed at Strasburg by Pryss, in the year
1488, in quarto. The work itself belongs
to a much earlier date, having been written
in 1332 by a monk, Hugo von Reutlingen,
whose real name is believed to have been
Spechtshart. It consists of a Latin poem
of six hundred and thirty-five hexameter
verses, which are also leonine. The
book is a fine specimen of Gothic type.
The poem itself is printed in a bold
letter, and continuously, with no separa-
tion of the lines beyond the fact that each
begins with a capital, and it is accompanied
with an elaborate commentary in smaller
type, the author of which is unknown.

It is divided into four Books, which treat of Gamut, of the Monochord, of Intervals, and of the Church Tones and their use, and it was designed as an assistance to the younger clergy in the proper discharge of their duties. These are not easy matters to explain in prose, but the difficulty is greatly increased when the medium is verse. It is, therefore, not wonderful that occasionally the poem without the commentary is wholly unintelligible. No doubt, the object was to impress the rules of the art on the memory, in the same way that in the old days of the Eton Latin Grammar one learned *Propria quæ maribus* and *As in præsenti.* The reader may be glad to see a specimen. This is part of the description of the mono-chord :—

"Pythagoras factor   cujus fuit atque repertor.
Istum doctorem   tibi præstant concava ligna,
Cum sola chorda   magadis apte sociata
Ad quas stet scripta   per claves schedula longa,
Quæ claves veras   præstent ex ordine formas."

We have put spaces to show the rhyme between the first and second half of the line. "Magada" is the "bridge" of a lyre.

The volume is of great rarity, but a copy is to be found at the British Museum, and a reprint of it, with a translation both of the poem and of the commentary, in German, with preface and notes by Carl Beck, Dean of Reutlingen, forms Vol. lxxxix. of the *Bibliothek des Litterarischen Verein in Stuttgart* (Stuttgart, 1868 : 8vo).

The next work to be noted is the equally rare *Lilium Musice Plane* of Michael Keinspeck (Basel, 1496 : 4to), of which there are several editions, followed in 1501 by the *Opus Aureum* of Nicolaus Wollick, *Impressum Colonie per honestum virum Henricum Quentel, Anno missionis in carnem divini verbi millesimo quingentesimo uno addito* (quarto), with two subsequent editions. The purpose of most of the books on Music which now began to be published in rapid succession was the instruction of ecclesiastics in the proper rendering of the musical part of divine worship. Secular music was scarcely considered worthy of serious treatment. These all follow much the same plan, treating of the elements of Music, Gregorian Plain-Song and the definition of the eight tones, with the rules of measurable Music and of counterpoint. Of such treatises it will suffice to mention

the *Tetrachordon* of Cochlœus (Nuremberg,
1507 : 4to), of which there are later editions, the *Clarissima plane atque choralis
Musice Interpretatio* of Praspergius (Basel,
1507 : 4to), the *Opusculum Musices*
of Simon de Quercu (a Belgian, whose
real name was Duchesne) (Nuremberg,
1513 : 4to), and the *Musicæ Institutiones*
of Othmar Nachtigall, (Strasburg, 1515 :
4to), all in the Latin language; while
Martin Agricola brought out *Ein Kurtz
Deudsche Musica* (Wittemberg, 1528 : 8vo)
and his *Musica figuralis Deudsch* (*ib.*,
1532 : 8vo), both printed by George
Rhaw.   With these may be mentioned
a number of still smaller didactic works,
in the form of primers or catechisms,
of which the most popular was the
Enchiridion of George Rhaw, the printer
of Wittemberg, which was reprinted many
times between the years 1518 and 1553.
This is a primer intended for the boys in
the school of Wittemberg, but Rhaw
published also a catechism drawn up by
Spangenberg for the school of Nordhausen,
the editions of which are also numerous.

In the *Rerum Musicarum Opusculum* of
Froschius (Strasburg, 1635 : folio) the
author indulges in many speculations; but
the book is noticeable for the beautiful
printing of the examples by Peter Schœffer

and Mathias Apiarius, the latter of whom afterwards carried on business alone in Berne, where he published a *Compendium Musices* by Lampadius (1537 : 8vo). The *Ars Canendi* of Sebaldus Heyden (Nuremberg, 1537 : 4to), apart from its merits as a treatise, is valuable for the examples which it contains of the works of Obrecht, Josquin de Près, Senfel, Heinrich Isaac, and others, which are not to be found elsewhere.

But German—or perhaps we should rather say Swiss—musical scholarship was best represented by Henricus Loris, or Loritus, better known as Glareanus, from his birth in the Canton of Glarus. He was a man of vast general acquirements, was crowned poet-laureate in 1512 for his poem in honour of the Emperor Maximilian I., and lived on terms of intimacy with Erasmus and other learned men of the time. His edition of Boethius has already been mentioned, but he made other valuable additions to the literature of Music. His first work was his *Isagoge in Musicen* (4to), published without place, printer's name, or date, but from the dedication it appears to have been brought out at Basle in 1516. The work is ornamented with a title-page by Holbein and differs little from other rudimentary works of the time.   The reputation of Glareanus rests on a work of much greater importance, his *Dodecachordon* (Basel, 1547 : folio).   The student of musical history will remember that St. Ambrose recognised four Church modes, while St. Gregory extended the number to eight.   The object of the treatise of Glareanus is to prove that there were actually twelve modes, and that they are identical with the ancient Greek modes, rejecting the Locrian and Hypolocrian as unavailable. Apart from the importance of the work as a theoretical treatise, it has other claims on the gratitude of musicians, on account of the numerous examples it contains of the works of the older musicians, such as Josquin de Près, H. Isaac, Okenheim, Pierre de la Rue, and others.   An epitome of this work in Latin was produced at Basle in 1557 and 1559 (small square 8vo) and a German translation of the epitome in similar form at Basle in 1559, both probably by Viconegger (Woneggar).

The *Musice active Micrologus* (Leipzig, 1517 : obl. 4to) of Ornithoparcus (Vogelsang), a treatise on all the different branches of musical knowledge, received the honour of translation into English at the hands of the eminent lutenist John Dowland (London, 1609 : folio).   Both the original and the translation are of considerable rarity and interest, the outspoken quaintness of the original losing none of its vigour in the translation. It is from this work that comes the often-quoted passage " The English doe carroll ; the French sing ; the Spaniards weepe ; the Italians which dwell about the coasts of Janua (Genoa?) caper with their voyces ; the others barke ; but the Germanes (which I am ashamed to utter) doe howle like Wolves."

In France, works on Music do not appear to have been so numerous. The earliest is a little treatise by J. Faber Stapulensis (Le Febvre, of Étaples). Fétis says that the first edition was published in Paris in 1496, folio, under the title of *Elementa Musicalia*, and that he bought a copy in London ; no such volume, however, is to be found in the catalogue of his library. It was reprinted by H. Stephanus, Paris, 1510, and again in 1514, in the latter case together with a treatise on Arithmetic by Nemorarius, and other works. The last edition, *Musica libris quatuor demonstrata*, was printed in Paris by Cavellat (1551 : 4to). The only other work which seems to have met with any vogue was the *Utilissime musicales regule* of Guerson, first published at Paris in the

early years of the sixteenth century. Fétis
quotes two other editions—Paris, 1509, and
ib., 1513, both small quarto, in Gothic type.
The writer's copy is dated 1510 and probably differs only in date from the edition
of 1509. Throughout the work the
initials and headings of the chapters are
printed in red, as are the staves of the
musical examples.

In Spain musical scholarship was up-
held by the *De Musica Libri Septem* of
Franciscus Salinas (Salamanca, 1577 :
folio). The author was blind from his
early years, but succeeded in acquiring
a profound knowledge of Music and the
command of an admirable Latin style.
Twenty-three years of his life were passed
in Rome, but he returned to Salamanca
to become professor at the University,
where his work was published as a text-
book for his lectures. The first Book
treats of musical ratios, the second of
intervals ; the third is occupied with the
ancient musical systems and the consideration of Temperament as applied to
instruments ; the fourth treats of the
teachings of Pythagoras and Aristoxenus,
with criticisms on Gaforius, Glareanus,
Zarlino, and others. The remaining books
are devoted to rhythm, both as applied
to Music and to Latin versification. These

are illustrated by many specimens of Spanish melodies.

As Music formed one of the seven liberal arts, it was of course treated of in the many works written in their explanation—generally in a very perfunctory manner. Among these we may mention as favourable specimens the *Somma di tutte le Scienze* of Aurelius Marinati (Rome, 1557 : 4to). And it is of course treated of in such encyclopædic works as the *De Expetendis, et Fugiendis Rebus Opus* of George Valla (Venice, Aldus 1501 ; 2 vols, folio), which a recent bibliographer describes as " two splendid volumes, with absolutely nothing interesting in them," and in the equally ponderous *Lectionum antiquarum Libri XXX* of L. Rhodoginus, also printed by Aldus in 1516, folio. It was reprinted in 1550 by Frobenius (Basel) in one volume folio of cclii. + 1182 pages. No wonder the printer adds a note—" *Opus hoc in duo volumina commodè secari poterit in ternione gg.*" !

The *Rosetum* of Joannes Mauburnus (Paris, 1510) is on a more merciful scale, for it is a quarto of about seven hundred pages only. It is doubtful whether this curious work should be included here, as its aim is religious rather than musical ; however, the author describes and gives figures of several musical instruments, but always with the view of drawing a moral lesson from them. He even contrives to extract spiritual comfort from the Guidonian Hand—which to many must have produced quite other feelings.

The respective merits of Plain-Song—where the notes simply followed the prosody of the words—and of the *Cantus Mensurabilis,* where the relative duration of the notes, governed by an elaborate and complicated system, was fixed by the notation—an obvious necessity as soon as harmony came into use—were warmly contested. A curious development of this discussion was the *Bellum Musicale inter plani et mensurabilis Cantus reges, de Principatu in Musicæ Provinciæ obtinendo, contendentes* of Claude Sebastian (Strasburg, 1563 : 4to). (The first edition is said to be 1553.) The work is rather a tedious allegory (as allegories are apt to be), describing the war between two kings, brothers, who reign over the adjacent kingdoms of Plain-Song and Mensurate Music. The King of Plain-Song finds many allies,—the Pope—the Cardinals—even the Lutheran ministers. The King of the Mensurates has under command his relatives, Mode, Time, and Prolation. Each army is composed of notes, and the shock of war is so violent that some of the notes receive black eyes! Plain-Song at first appears to be gaining the day, but victory is finally decided in favour of *Cantus Mensurabilis*. Peace is at last made between the rival sovereigns, and the limits of their respective empires finally settled. The book is scarce, but a German translation by Raymund Schlecht (reprinted from Cäcilia) was published at Treves in 1876, octavo.

Strange to say, a very similar allegory on the same subject was written many years later, although it may be convenient to speak of it here. The title of the work is *Belligerasmus, id est Historia belli exorti in Regno Musico* (Hamburg, 1622 : 8vo). The plot is almost identical with that of the former work; in this case Orpheus is the champion of Mensurate Music, Bisthon of Plain-Song. There is a curious literary question attached to this little book. It was published under the name of *Erasmus Sartorius*, and a second edition appeared in 1626. In 1637 Sartorius died, and in 1639 Lauremberg, a physician and poet of Rostock, republished the book, claiming to be the author. His claim has yet to be substantiated.

CHAPTER IV.

MUSICAL LITERATURE IN THE
SEVENTEENTH CENTURY.

N the early years of the seventeenth century was published a work on Music which, partly on account of its real value, and perhaps still more on account of its excessive rarity, has been surrounded with interest. This is *El Melopeo* of Pedro Cerone, which although written in Spanish was the work of an Italian and published at Naples in 1613, in a folio volume of about twelve hundred pages. The author, born at Bergamo, became a priest, and, visiting Spain, joined the Chapel Royal of Philip II. and his successor Philip III. The kingdom of Naples and that of Spain were then under the same ruler, and thus the services of Cerone were transferred to Naples, and there his book was published. It is supposed that the king must have

borne the whole or a part of the expense
of printing it, and that he made the use
of the Spanish language a condition of
his assistance. The tradition is that the
entire edition was shipped to Spain, that
the ship was wrecked and the whole of
the copies lost, with the exception of
thirteen which had been retained in
Naples. We are ignorant of the authority
for this story, but the work is undoubtedly
among the scarcest in musical literature.
Fétis speaks of the difficulties which both
he and Padre Martini met with in obtaining copies, and of the want of success
which attended Dr. Burney in the search.
One, however, was in the possession of
the late Mr. John Bishop, of Cheltenham,
and a magnificent copy is lying before
the writer as he pens this notice.

It is curious that, although possessing a
copy, Fétis should have given the author's
name wrongly as " Dominique Pierre," an
error followed by Grove's dictionary,
which calls him " Domenico Pietro."
The title stands *Compuesto por el R. D.*
Pedro Cerone—i.e., *el Reverendo Don*
Pedro Cerone. Domenico is a misreading
altogether, and this the dedicatory verses
fully confirm.

Fétis is also guilty of suggesting a
charge against the author for which there

seems to be no foundation whatever.
Cerone, like many learned men of that
period, although showing a vast erudition,
frequently allows his fancy to run away
with him, and becomes prolix and tedious,
so that the reader is tempted to believe
that two different writers have been concerned.   It appears that Zarlino in his
Sopplimenti announced his intention of
producing a work under the same title,
and Fétis is bold enough to start the idea
that Cerone may in some unexplained
way have become possessed of the manuscript and incorporated it in his own
book ; but the charge is absolutely un-
supported by evidence.   The book is
undoubtedly long-winded above the aver-
age.   It considers at great length the
moral qualities desirable in a musician,
the evil and the good caused by the use
of wine, and other such useless inquiries,
which fill the first two hundred pages of
the volume ; but when the author really
"buckles to" he is clear in his explanations, which cover the whole field of
musical knowledge.

We have now to speak of two writers
whose reputation extended far beyond
the limits of the musical world—both men
of wide and various learning, and of both
of whom it may be said, as in the case of

a modern scholar, that their "foible was omniscience."

The first of these was Père Marin Mersenne, of the order of Minims, the fellow-student of Descartes, the intimate friend of the elder Pascal, of Roberval and of Peiresc, the correspondent of all who were eminent among mathematicians, or in the pursuit of physical science. In those days scientific journalism was not invented; anything worthy of note was sure to be at once communicated to Mersenne, and as certain to be passed on to all who were likely to take interest in it—in fact, he may be said to have performed the functions of a "clearing house" of scientific information. His thirst for knowledge extended to all branches of learning, both theological and scientific, but his tastes led him to take a special interest in Music, with the result that his writings on that science form the larger part of his somewhat voluminous publications. It must be admitted that Mersenne was disposed to be over credulous. A little want of the critical faculty, possibly an occasional absence of common-sense, at times lead him into extravagances which we can afford to smile at, while admiring the powers of patient research, and the wide-spread knowledge, which rendered him the prominent figure in the musical literature of the first half of the seventeenth century.

Many of his works are far from common, and his most important one decidedly scarce, and frequently imperfect. It is, we suppose, for this reason that so many of the descriptions of them are incorrect —for instance, the article in Grove's *Dictionary*, although short and perfunctory, is a tissue of blunders ; the writer cannot have examined the works which he professes to describe. This is the more inexcusable as Fétis has done so with more than usual care and accuracy.

We have already spoken of Mersenne's *Quæstiones Celeberrimæ in Genesim.* Early in life he seems to have projected a vast work on his favourite subject, but was probably compelled to moderate his ambition by the difficulty of finding a publisher willing to risk so serious a venture. At any rate, for several years he contented himself by bringing out a series of small works, each embracing a portion only of the subject. The first of these was his *Traité de L'Harmonie Universelle. Où est contenu la Musique Theorique et Pratique des Anciens and Modernes, avec les causes de ses effets,*

(Paris, 1627: 8vo). This work was not published under his own name, but professes to be written by le Sieur de Sermes. The work begins with a summary of the projected sixteen Books on Music; the volume itself, of four hundred and eighty-seven pages, contains only the first two of these, Book I. containing, in the words of our author, "that which is taught by Euclid, Ptolemy, Bacchius, Boethius, Guido d'Arezzo, Faber, Glareanus, Folianus, Zarlino, Salinas, Galilei, l'Illuminato (Illuminato Aiguino, of Brescia, who published a book on Plain-Song, Venice, 1562: 4to), Cerone, etc, and many other things which have not been treated of up to the present time." Book II. considers the relations of sounds, of consonances, of rhythm, and runs off into very characteristic flights of fancy—for instance, that the proportions of Solomon's Temple are based on the application of the laws of musical harmony. Not the least curious part of this curious book is the following note on the last page :—"*Achevé d'imprimer l'an de la période de Scaliger 6342, du monde 5612, and de Jésus Christ 1618, que les autres croyent estre le 1634 ou 1635.*"

This was followed by the *Questions*

Harmoniques (Paris, 1634 : 8vo). No author's name appears on the title, but the privilege is granted to the R.P.M.R.M. (*i.e.*, Revérend Père Marin Mersenne), and the dedication is signed F.M. While still intended as a prelude to a larger work, this volume forms no part of the sixteen Books of which the syllabus is given in the *Traité*. It addresses itself to the following questions :—

1. Whether Music is agreeable, whether men of learning should take pleasure in it, and what should be thought of those who do not like it, or who dislike it, or even hate it.

2. Whether Music is a science, and is governed by fixed and ascertainable principles. In the course of this investigation he prints the *Discours Sceptique sur la Musique* of La Mothe le Vayer, without any clue to its origin. It had been communicated to Mersenne by its author.

3. Whether the learned in Music are better judges of the excellence of airs, etc., than those who are ignorant of Music.

4. Whether the practice of Music is preferable to the theory, and whether more should be thought of one who knows only how to compose, or to sing, than of one who knows only the scientific part of Music.

In his next work, *Les Préludes de l'Harmonie Universelle* (Paris, 1634 : 8vo), his fantastic nature fairly runs away with him, as the reader will see. In the first chapter the author considers what should be the horoscope of the perfect musician, and he proceeds to cast the nativity of such a person calculated for the latitude of Paris. He has to admit with regret that he would be of short life, and meet with a violent end. It is a relief to find two alternative horoscopes of " a very perfect musician," which are apparently not open to this objection. Having seriously given these nativities, he proceeds at great length to inquire whether any credence whatever is to be given to Judicial Astronomy, and arrives at the conclusion that if human beings are influenced by the stars, the knowledge of it is reserved to God, and that man cannot reasonably desire to penetrate it. To this somewhat lame conclusion he arrives after wasting a hundred and nine pages over the question.

He then proceeds to consider what should be the temperament of the perfect musician. The reader would probably find it difficult in these days to get his nativity cast, but he may be glad to know whether his temperament promises

success in the art.   To our great regret
we cannot enlighten him, for Mersenne
adduces the merits of each in succession
with such judicial fairness that he confesses himself quite unable to arrive at
any decision on the point.   Space fails
to go through the entire work, but he
reverts to the question whether the ear
or the intellect should be the judge of
excellence in a musical composition, and
then, descending to practical matters,
describes experiments made to decide
in what part musical strings equal in
length and thickness would break when
stretched by equal forces.

He still kept his projected work steadily
in view, and in 1635 succeeded in finding
a publisher for his *Harmonicorum Libri
XII.* (Paris : folio).   Fétis gives this date,
but his own copy is dated 1636 ; it appears
however, that the " Privilege " was granted
as early as 1629, so we may assume that
the work was probably completed, although
not printed, in that year.   The arrangement of the Books is different, but with the
works already described the ground previously mapped out in the sixteen Books
of his *Traité* of 1627 is virtually covered.
It is not to be supposed that the author
could entirely curb his active imagination,
but on the whole he succeeded in keeping

much closer to his subject. An examination of the work will at once show how much it was in advance of anything published up to that time, and it is the first in which the science of acoustics is applied practically to the study of Music. Perhaps to us in the present day the greatest interest is in the last four Books, treating of the various instruments known at that time, divided into stringed and wind instruments (the organ having a book to itself) and instruments of percussion, as bells and drums. These are illustrated profusely with woodcuts, as well as with engravings on copper, both printed in the text. It is worthy of notice that in treating of the organ, several schemes are given for dividing the octave into more than twelve semi-tones, so as to be able to use it in keys impossible with unequal temperament.

Having published this treatise in 1636, it is not a little remarkable that in the same year he at last fulfilled the wish of his life, by bringing out the first part of his great work under the title of *Harmonie Universelle.* It was printed in Paris by Sebastian Cramoisy, who deserves to have his name recorded for his enterprise in venturing to undertake so enormous a work—upwards of fifteen hundred pages folio—filled with woodcuts and engravings, those, however, in the *Harmonicorum Libri XII.* doing duty again. A note is appended, stating that the musical examples are printed by Pierre Ballard, as was also the case in the former work. This was rendered necessary by the fact that Ballard (and his descendants for many years after) had the exclusive right of printing music in France.

It would take too much of our space to give an analysis of this work. In the main it follows the arrangement of its Latin predecessor, but it is misleading to speak of it as a translation. The subjects are treated much more exhaustively, and on the whole the author keeps more closely to his text. But there is no lack of unexplainable wanderings from it. Between Books III. and IV. he prints a *Traité de Mécanique* by his friend Roberval which has no connexion whatever with Music. The Book on instruments of percussion winds up—if not without rhyme, without reason—with a long versification of the Athanasian Creed! This is followed by several pages of *errata* and *addenda*, concluding with an Essay on the moral lessons to be drawn from Pure Mathematics.

Scattered through the book are many

examples taken from the works of musicians not to be found elsewhere, which of course are of great historical interest. With all its faults it is a rich storehouse of musical information, which has been freely drawn upon by many of the author's successors. On the strength of a statement of De Bure it has the reputation of being the rarest work in musical literature. No doubt, comparatively few copies would be called for of a book appealing to a limited public, and which must have been at all times costly. Copies of it undoubtedly fetch a high price in the present day, but many musical works are of much greater rarity. The collation is exceedingly difficult, as the pagination frequently recommences, on no apparent system.

It remains to be said that in 1648 Mersenne brought out a second edition of his *Harmonicorum Libri XII.*, but whether this is a complete reprint the writer is unable to say ; also that the *Cogitata-physico-mathematica* (Paris, 1644 : 2 vols., 4to), contains four books on " Harmonia "—*i.e.*, Music, sandwiched between a treatise on Navigation and one on Mechanics, in which several of the figures from his other works are used.

When a young man of twenty-two years,

Descartes—the lifelong friend of Mersenne—wrote, to please a friend, a short treatise on the mathematical proportions of musical intervals. Feeling a want of sufficient practical knowledge, he would never consent to its publication; it was, however, printed after his death under the title of *Compendium Musicæ* (Utrecht, 1650: 4to), and from that time was included in the collected edition of his works. This little book was twice translated, firstly into English as *Renatus Descartes' Excellent Compendium of Musick: with Necessary and Judicious Animadversions Thereupon, By a person of Honour*, who was Lord Brouncker, the first president of the Royal Society (London, 1653 : 4to). The other translation was into French by the Abbé Poisson (Paris, 1668 : 4to), also with some elucidations by the translator.

We must not dismiss French writers on Music without mentioning the work of the eminent engineer Solomon de Caus : *Institution Harmonique, Divisée en deux parties, En la première sont monstrées les proportions des intervalles harmoniques, Et en la deuxième les compositions dicelles* (Frankfort, 1615 : folio), a work which would be worthy of note if only on account of its admirable printing.

Germany possessed almost an exact

counterpart of Mersenne in the famous Jesuit, Father Athanasius Kircher, a man of the most wide-reaching knowledge, with the most insatiable desire to increase it. Natural Science, the study of ancient and oriental languages, Antiquity, Music, all had attractions for him. He was one of the first to form a Museum, which has been often described and is still to be seen in Rome. His entire works number over thirty, some in several volumes, most of them in folio. His learning was probably as great as that of Mersenne, and it will scarcely be wronging him to admit that he was equally credulous.

His earliest work was on the subject of Magnetism, which would not appear to have much connexion with Music. His *Magnes, sive de Arte Magnetica opus tripartitum* (first published in Rome, 1641 : 4to; but more commonly met with in the folio edition of 1654) contains, however, a chapter on the magnetic influence of Music, and then proceeds to consider the effect of the bite of the tarantula spider, the evil results of which he attributes to magnetic influence, to be cured by dancing alone. He gives the music in use for that purpose, which bears no resemblance to that known as a tarantella in the present day.

His great work, the *Musurgia Univer-salis* (Rome, 1650 : 2 vols., folio), is on a scale but slightly smaller than the *Harmonie Universelle* of Mersenne, and, like it, the plan of the work covers the whole field of musical knowledge. Something, no doubt, it owes to its predecessor, but it has an independent interest of its own. After some general remarks on sound, the author proceeds to give a description of the organs both of hearing and speech, in man and in other animals, giving the songs of several birds in musical nota-tion, and explaining the production of sound by insects. He then treats of the music of the Jews and the Greeks, the proportions of intervals, the theories of Boethius and Guido d'Arezzo, with the explanation of the Guidonian Hand and of the use of the monochord. This brings us to Book V., which contains the famous *Nodus Salomonis*, a canon originally com-posed by Pietro Valentini to be sung by ninety-six voices arranged in twenty-four choirs. Kircher rightly describes it as " *verius Labyrinthum*," and then proceeds to improve on it by showing that it could be sung by twelve million two hundred thousand voices, disposed in three million two hundred thousand choirs—that all the men in Italy, Spain, Germany, or France, would barely suffice for its performance, which would last two hundred and thirty-two days, allowing no interval for refreshment or sleep!

After this solemn trifling the learned Jesuit gives an excellent description of the different instruments then in use. He goes at length into the question of the necessity of additional notes to the octave in instruments having fixed tones, and on this point he is largely indebted to Mersenne, from whose work many of the figures are copied. Rhythm and Accent come in for a large share of attention, and then his love of the marvellous begins to run away with him; we have disquisitions on the curative effects of Music, our old friend the tarantula makes a further appearance, we are taught how harmony is exemplified in the construction of the human form, and a system of secret writing by means of musical notes. The Harmony of the Spheres comes in for attention, several musical automata are described, and, lastly, the construction of the Æolian Harp, of which Kircher was probably the inventor.

Unlike the *Harmonie Universelle* of Mersenne, this work is by no means uncommon, and with all its faults—perhaps partly on account of them—is a book which may be always consulted with pleasure. It should be added that an epitome of the work in German was made by Andreas Hirsch, a Protestant minister, under the title of *Kircherus Jesuita Germanus Germaniæ redonatus* (Hall [in Swabia], 1662 : sm. 8vo), the value of which is greatly diminished by a total absence of illustrations.

The consideration of the phenomena of Echoes formed a portion of the *Musurgia*. Kircher returned to this subject at greater length in his *Phonurgia nova* (Kempten, 1673 : folio). He explains with great detail the principles of the reflection of Sound, and describes his own original experiments to ascertain the rate at which it travels. The musical properties of tubes, both cylindrical and conical, are expounded, and the reasons of the imperfect scales of such instruments. The plan adopted by the ancients of building vases into the walls of their theatres is described at length, and he then proceeds to give descriptions of some of the most famous echoes known to him. He then applies the principles he has enunciated to the contrivance of what he conceives to be works of practical utility—for instance, how a room may be constructed so that whatever is said in it may be distinctly heard in another chamber, or how two people at a distance, and unable to see each other, may yet be able to indulge in conversation ; and he anticipates the *resonators* which have been used with such results by Helmholtz in his researches. Among many other curious inquiries, he investigates the reasons of the fall of the walls of Jericho, which he concludes must have been miraculous. The book is a beautiful specimen of printing, and profusely illustrated, both with woodcuts and copperplate engravings. It was translated into German under the title of *Neue Hall-und Thou-Kunst* (Nordlingen, 1684 : folio) by Agathus Cario, a pseudonym which remains unexplained. The cuts and engravings are much less artistic than those in the original edition.

The similarity between the two previous writers has induced us to pass over a book of earlier date, unfortunately of very great rarity—the *Syntagma Musicum* of Michael Prætorius, a musician of whom little is known apart from the voluminous compositions which he has left, and the bare facts that he was born in 1571 and died on his fiftieth birthday in 1621 at Wolfenbüttel, having filled the posts of Kapellmeister at Luneburg, and after-

wards of organist, Kapellmeister and
secretary to the Duke of Brunswick, and
that he was in orders.   There can be no
doubt that his real name was Schulz =
magistrate, of which Prætorius was the
received Latinity.   From his book one
may judge him to have been an earnest-
minded, plodding man, of ample knowledge, not without the fair share of pedantry
which becomes a German of that date.
It was the author's intention to have completed the work in four volumes, but
unfortunately death overtook him before
the completion of the last.   Of these
volumes the first is in Latin and was
published at Wittemberg in the year
1615, in quarto.   It is divided into two
parts, the first treating of sacred music
among the Jews, with an account of the
musical instruments mentioned in the
Bible, tracing the history of Music down
to the Romish Church, with a description
of the music of the Mass and other offices.
The second part is devoted to the secular
music and musical instruments of the
ancients.

The second volume is entitled *De
Organographia*, and was published at
Wolfenbüttel in 1619.   In it he drops the
use of the Latin language and writes in
German.   It consists of a description of

the various instruments in use at that time, and it is on this that the principal value of the work at the present day depends. It is accompanied by a *Theatrum Instrumentorum, seu Sciographia* (Wolfenbüttel, 1620) containing excellent wood-engravings of the instruments described in the text. This is of the greatest interest, and fortunately has been admirably reproduced by the Gesellschaft für Musikforschung, Berlin, 1882.

The third volume, which is also in German, and published at Wolfenbüttel in 1619, treats of contemporary music in Italy, France, England, and Germany, and of the different forms of composition in use. The only Englishman mentioned seems to be Thomas Morley, and his name appears in a list of composers only. It then proceeds to give a description of notation, the modes, and transposition, with an explanation of Italian musical terms, the arrangement of a vocal and instrumental concert, as well as instructions in the true way of training choir-boys in the Italian manner. The volume closes with a very interesting list of his numerous musical works already published, or "*mit Göttlicher Hülfe*" still to be published, "*so im der liebe Gott das Leben fristet.*" But this was not to be.

The author was not even able to complete his great work, the fourth volume of which was to have been devoted to the explanation of the rules of counterpoint. The dates and descriptions have been taken from an excellent and complete copy in the writer's possession ; but an article in Grove's *Dictionary* ("Syntagma," vol. iv., p. 44), by Mr. W. S. Rockstro, proves that there was an earlier edition of the second and third volumes, as shown by typographical differences.

The German works of this period are distinguished by their pedantry, and by the length of their titles, which forbids us to transcribe them in full. We must, however, mention the *Musica Prattica* of Herbst (Nuremberg, 1642), the same writer's *Musica Poetica* (*ib.*, 1643), and the *Arte Practica e Poetica* (Frankfort, 1653) all in quarto, and written in German, in spite of the first words of the title, which in each case is continued in a barbarous jumble of languages.

But for pedantry and elephantine wit, the name of Wolfgang Caspar Printz, von Waldthurm, as he invariably describes himself, from the place of his birth, stands unrivalled. His best and most useful work is undoubtedly his *Historische Beschreibung*, to be spoken of later. The book, however, by which he is best known is probably his *Phrynis Mytilenæus oder Satyrischer Componist*, two parts of which were published successively at Quedlinburg, in 1676 and 1677, in quarto. But these were reprinted, together with a third Book, at Dresden, also in quarto, in the year 1696. The work is a satire against ignorant and incompetent composers who presume to teach others. Phrynis of Mytilene was a musician of antiquity, who in this work is supposed to have been placed with a modern master to learn his art. The style is heavy and tedious, and the wit cumbrous. Printz published other works, but several awaiting publication were burned in a fire which destroyed his house, and the greater part of the town of Sorau, where he lived. He tells us that this misfortune had the effect of impairing his memory—it certainly saved the world several prolix and tedious treatises.

Literary activity appears to have ceased in Italy during this century, perhaps because the musicians were more usefully occupied in composition; but the innovations of Monteverde, that great originator of the modern school of music, were not suffered to pass without a protest. In 1600 Giovanni Maria Artusi, already

known by a treatise on counterpoint, published the first instalment of his *Artusi,
overo delle Imperfettioni della Moderna
Musica* (Venice : folio). Artusi was an
uncompromising advocate of the old
order of things, and his book, which
takes the form of a dialogue between
Luca and Vario, is a protest against the
use of unprepared sevenths and ninths,
although he indulges in frequent digres-
sions into other subjects of interest. A
continuation was published in Venice in
1603, also folio. The controversy was
revived more than forty years later by a
royal disputant, John IV., King of Portugal,
in his *Defensa de la Musica Moderna
contra la errada opinion del obispo
Cyrillo Franco*, published anonymously
(at Lisbon in 1649 (?) : 4to), the authorship
of which, however, is well authenticated.
An Italian translation, also without place
or date, appeared later.

The *Organo Suonarino* of Banchieri
(Venice, 1605 : 4to) was often reprinted, having been one of the first
books to give instructions for playing
from a figured Bass. Treatises on Plain-
Song, a knowledge of which formed a
necessary part of the education of every
priest, appeared in rapid succession. In
1657 Avella produced his *Regole di*

Musica . . . e molte cose nuove e curiose
(Rome: folio), the interest of which will
be found in the "new and curious matters" rather than in the Rules. He
treats of the relation between Music and
the motions of the stars, and gives some
good advice to singers, especially on the
preservation of the voice, recommending
them to mix water with their wine in
summer, but to drink it neat in winter.
The first edition of *Li Primi Albori
Musicali* of Lorenzo Penna appeared
in 1656 (Bologna: 4to). The work,
several times reprinted, is a treatise on
the general principles of music and
counterpoint, while the third part teaches
the principles of playing the organ or
harpsichord "*sopra la parte*"—*i.e.*, the art
of accompanying from the figured bass.

The works of Berardi, a notice of which
will conclude our remarks on Italian publications during the seventeenth century,
prove how Music was losing the fine
traditions of Palestrina and his school in
the search after ingenious contrivances
with which Art had no connexion. His
first work, *Ragionamenti Musicali* (Bologna, 1681: 12mo), was in the form of
a dialogue, actually written by Giuseppe
Orsolini, a Bass of the Cathedral of
Spoleto, of which Berardi was Maestro

di Capella, based on his oral teaching. The contents are very miscellaneous, treating of musicians from Tubal Cain to Palestrina, attributing the invention of the violin to Orpheus, and of the bow to Sappho—in short, the work is more amusing than useful.

His *Documenti Armonici* (Bologna, 1687 : 4to) consists of explanations of the various ingenious contrivances which the taste of the time introduced into counterpoint, fugue, and canon—a book, no doubt, of vast learning, sadly misapplied. The *Miscellanea Musicale* (Bologna, 1689 : 4to), after some speculative matter, settles down to an explanation of the rules of counterpoint. The *Arcani Musicali* (Bologna, 1690 : 4to) perhaps exemplifies most completely the taste of the day, being wholly devoted to mechanical contrivances such as the "*canon cancrizans*"—which could be read backwards, as a crab is supposed to run— duets which could be sung whether the book was held upwards or downwards, and such other abstruse trifling. His last work, the *Perche Musicale* (Bologna, 1693 : 4to), consists of letters to friends explaining various points of musical interest.

The first English contribution to the

literature of Music of sufficient importance
to be noticed here is Thomas Morley's
well-known *Plaine and Easie Introduction
to Practicall Musicke, set downe in forme
of a Dialogue* (London, 1597 : folio ;
reissued with a new title in 1608). The
introduction has been so often quoted
that it must be familiar to most readers
—how Polymathes, "supper being ended
and Musicke books brought to the table,"
had to confess his inability to take his
part, so that the next day he lost no time
in seeking Master Gnorimus to repair the
defects of his education. The work
carries us through the course of instruction, which is given with much clearness ;
and any one desiring to master the complicated time-table of that day, with its
greater and lesser prolations, cannot have
a better guide. It contains many examples of interest, and a list of previous
writers and composers who have been
consulted. A proof of the popularity of
the work, and of the diligence with which
it has been studied, is the battered and
thumbed state of most of the copies
which are met with. The work was
reprinted as late as the year 1771.

That Music was considered to form
part of a liberal education is also proved
by the fact that a chapter on it is included

in the *Compleat Gentleman* of Henry
Peacham (London, 1622 : quarto).   After
praising Henry VIII. and other noble
persons for their devotion to the art, he
proceeds to characterise some of the
principal composers of the day.   " For
Motets and Musick of Piety and Devotion . . . I prefer above all other our
Phœnix Mr. William Byrd, whom in
that kind, I know not whether any may
equall, I am sure none excell."   Vittoria,
Luca Marenzio, Orazio Vecchi, Giovanni
Croce, and other foreign composers, receive commendation, and he speaks
according to knowledge, for he is able
to recommend special works by them ; but
while he rightly admires these writers, it
is pleasant to find him speaking of Douland,
Morley, Wilbye, Weelkes, East, Bateson,
and others of our noble body of
madrigal writers, as " inferior to none in
the world (how much soever the Italian
attributes to himself) for depth of skill,
and richness of conceit."   Several editions
of this work appeared.

We have already mentioned Douland's
translation of *Ornithoparcus his Micrologus*.
In 1636 appeared a curious book, *The
Principles of Musick, In singing and setting : With the twofold use thereof ; [Eccles-
iasticall and Civil*], " by the Rev. Charles

Butler (London, 1636 : 4to). It is an
excellent little practical treatise on Music ;
the remarkable point about it is that the
author was an early, probably the first,
adopter of phonetic spelling, which he
had already used in a previous work, *The
feminin˙ Monarchi˙ or the Histori˙ of Bees*
(Oxford, 1634 : 4to), a book which also
has a slight musical interest as containing
a description of the music of Bees when
swarming, which the author has arranged as
a "Melissomelos, or Bees' Madrigall." His
system of phonetics involved the casting
of some special type : for instance, *h* following a consonant is always represented by a
stroke through it. The initial *th* of *the*,
this, *that*, etc. is always represented by *d*
with a stroke. This and other eccen-
tricities give the book what Mr. Butler
calls an *od* appearance.

In this century were published two
handbooks of the art of Music, both of
which enjoyed remarkable popularity.
The first in the field, and the more
popular, was Playford's *Introduction to the
Skill of Musick. In two Books. First,
A brief and plain Introduction to Musick,
both for singing and for playing on the
Violl. By J. P. Second, The Art of
Setting or Composing of Musick in Parts
by a most familiar and easie Rule of*

*Counterpoint.   Formerly published by Dr.
Tho. Campion* : *but now republished with
large   Annotations   by   Mr.   Cristoph.
Sympson, and other Additions* (London,
1655 : 8vo).   This passed for many years
as the first edition, till the late Dr.
Rimbault came into the possession of a
copy dated 1654—the only one known—
which at his sale in 1877 was knocked
down for ten guineas.   Numerous editions
of this work, with alterations and additions,
were issued, the last, purporting to be
the nineteenth, in 1730; but there are
five or six unnumbered editions.   To the
seventh (1674) " The order of Perform-
ing the Divine Service in Cathedrals and
Collegiate   Chappels"   was   added ; it
appears in all subsequent editions, with
the exception of the twelfth and thirteenth,
(1694,   1697).   In   the   tenth   edition
(1683) Campion's " Art of Setting " dis-
appears, and is replaced by a " Brief
Introduction to the Art of Descant or
Composing Musick in Parts."   No author's
name is affixed to this, but it is afterwards
stated to be " with the additions of the
late Mr. Henry Purcell."   Each edition
contains a portrait of the author, of which
there are five variations.

In 1665 Christopher Simpson (or
Sympson, for he used both spellings),

who had a hand in the earlier editions of Playford's *Introduction*, brought out a handbook of his own under the title of *The Principles of Practical Musick* (London, 1665 : 8vo) which in the second and subsequent editions he changed to *A Compendium of Practical Musick in Five Parts.* 1. *The Rudiments of Song.* 2. *The Principles of Composition.* 3. *The Use of Discords.* 4. *The Form of Figurative Descant.* 5. *The Contrivance of Canon.* Eight editions were published in rapid succession, the last of which is dated 1732. They all contain a portrait, drawn and engraved by Faithorne, printed from the same plate. Many years afterwards a ninth and last edition (about 1760 ?) was brought out in oblong quarto.

Simpson had already won his spurs as a writer on Music by his *Division Violist : or an Introduction to the Playing upon a Ground* (London, 1659 : folio), of which Playford was the publisher. The dedication to Sir Robert Bolles, stating that it was " chiefly contrived . . . for the instruction of your little son," is very quaint. After describing the kind of viol and bow " fittest for Division," with a very characteristic full-page engraving of a gentleman in hat and wig, wearing very square-toed shoes on his very carefully turned-out feet, engaged in playing divisions, he proceeds to explain the mysteries of the art, appending a number of examples.

A second edition appeared in 1667— no longer published by "honest John Playford," with whom we hope he had not quarrelled in consequence of the publication of the rival elementary work already described. Sir Robert Bolles's "then little son" had grown to manhood and succeeded to his father's estate. To him it is dedicated, for the reasons that "you were the chief Occasion of the Book, . . . for it was contriv'd and carried on for Your Instruction in Musick. . . . And as it was made for You, so it has made You (by your ingenuity) not only the greatest Artist, but also the ablest Judge of it, that (I think) is this day in Europe ; (I mean) of a Gentleman, and no Professor of the science." It appears that Sir John Bolles produced such an effect in Rome by his playing, as witnessed by a copy of Latin verses addressed to him on the occasion, that his old instructor decided on issuing, with the assistance of his "own honoured Friend (and sometime Scholar in Musick), Mr. William Marsh" a Latin translation, side by side with the English work, "that

it might be understood in Foreign Parts."
Perhaps out of regard to the superior
politeness of foreigners, the gentleman
who is playing the divisions has removed
his hat. The plate is otherwise identical.
A third edition was published in 1712.
Both the second and third editions
contain a portrait of the author painted
by Carwarden, admirably engraved by
Faithorne.

In 1664 John Birchensha, an Irishman,
who describes himself as "Philomath"
published a translation (London : 8vo) of
the *Elementale Musicum* of "the learned
and famous Johannes Henricus Alstedius,"
originally produced at Frankfort in 1611.
As the production of a man signing himself "Philomath" it is not surprising to
meet with a fair share of pedantry. A
more important work is Matthew Locke's
*Melothesia, or Certain General Rules for
playing upon a Continued Bass* (London :
obl. 4to)—the first treatise on the subject
published in this country.

A most delightful book, Thomas Mace's
*Musick's Monument ; or a Remembrancer
of the Best Practical Musick, both Divine
and Civil, that has ever been known to
have been in the World*, appeared in 1676
(London : folio). The reader is puzzled
which to admire most, the fervour and

enthusiasm of the author, or the quaintness of his style, with his fondness for long compound words. On account of the interest of the book, even to the non-musical reader, and perhaps also for its excellent portrait of the author engraved by Faithorne, it is much sought for; copious quotations from it, however, will be found in Southey's *Doctor*, which no doubt has helped to increase its popularity.

The book is divided into three parts, the first of which treats of Music in Parochial and Cathedral Churches. He gives a description of the highest form of psalm singing. The Loyal City of York was in 1644 undergoing a siege, and our author, with "abundance of People of the *best Rank and Quality*—viz., *Lords*, *Knights* and *Gentlemen* of the Countries round about, besides the *Souldiers* and *Citizens*," went constantly to the Cathedral on Sunday; "and indeed their Number was so *exceeding great* that the *Church* was (as I may say) even *cramming* or *squeezing full*. Now here you must take notice, that they had then a *Custom in that Church* that always before the *Sermon* the *whole Congregation sang a Psalm*, together with the *Quire* and the *organ*; And you must also know, that there was a most *Excellent-large-plump-lusty-*

full-speaking Organ, which cost (as I am credibly informed) a *thousand pounds.*

"This *Organ,* I say, being let out, into all its *Fulness of Stops,* together with the *Quire* began the *Psalm.*

"But when that *Vast-Conchording-Unity* of the whole *Congregational-Chorus,* came (as I may say) *Thundering in,* even so, as it made the very *Ground shake* under us ; (*Oh the unutterable ravishing Soul's delight!*) In the which I was so *transported,* and *wrapt* up into *High Contemplations,* that there was no room left in *my whole Man,* viz. *Body, Soul, and Spirit,* for anything below *Divine* and *Heavenly Raptures.*"

We have no room for further quotation, but we think we have given enough to show the charm of the volume. The second book is the *Noble Lute made Easie,* and consists of the praise of that instrument, its proper care and management, the best way to repair accidental injuries, the method of fingering, and an explanation of the English lute tablature. His instructions as to the management of the instrument are very clear and practical. To keep the lute in the best order for playing, he recommends putting it " into a Bed that is constantly used, between the Rug and Blanket," but he is careful to add "That no Person be so inconsiderate as to Tumble down upon the Bed while the Lute is There."

The third part treats of "the Generous Viol," and also contains the plan of a "Musick-Roome, with Conveniency for severall Sorts of Auditors," and other musical contrivances.

Mace was one of the clerks of Trinity College, Cambridge, and apparently held in great respect by the University, for a large proportion of the subscribers to his book were members. Amongst these we notice the names of Drs. Barrow, Cudworth, and Isaac Newton. Sir Robert Bolles, the patron of Christopher Simpson, also appears in the list.

CHAPTER V.

The Musical Literature of the Eighteenth Century.

ONTINUING our chronological outline of the progress of Musical Literature, it will be seen that the eighteenth century was one of great advance, having been rendered illustrious by the work of Marpurg, Kirnberger, Mattheson and Forkel in Germany, Fux in Austria, Burney and Hawkins in England, Martini in Italy, Rameau and Rousseau in France.

Although the larger part of the works of Werckmeister appeared in the closing years of the previous century, it is convenient to speak here of his writings. His reputation rests more especially on his oftentimes reprinted little book on "Orgelprobe," or the art of examining an organ in all its departments, to ascertain whether the builder has honestly carried out his instructions. But in addition to this work, Werckmeister was a voluminous contributor to the literature of Music. His title-pages display all the pedantry of the time, and begin in Latin, proceeding in a mixture of German and Latin, while the works themselves are invariably in German. For instance, the title of his first theoretical work is *Musicæ Mathematicæ Hodegus Curiosus* (Frankfort, 1687 : 4to), which he proceeds to translate as *Richtiger Musicalischer Weg-Weiser.* It may be remarked that "Hodegus" is Greek and not Latin, and that the title continues to describe at great length the contents of the book, which is really a deduction of the ratios of the intervals of the scale from the division of the monochord. His *Hypomnemata Musica* (Quedlimburg, 1697 : 4to) treats of consonances and dissonances, while a considerable share of the book is devoted to the question of Temperament. The *Nothwendigsten Anmerckungen und Regeln wie der Bassus Continuus, oder General-Bass wol könne tractiret werden* (Aschersleben, 1698 : 4to) describes its own purpose, the writer having been content, for once, to use his own language. His *Cribrum Musicum* (Musical Sieve) (Quedlimburg, 1700 : 4to) consists of instructions for avoiding false progressions. His *Harmono-*

logia Musica (Frankfort, 1702 : 4to) is a handbook of single and double counterpoint, while his last work, *Musickalische Paradoxal-Discourse* (Quedlimburg, 1707 : 4to) is an examination into the causes of the decay of sound-music.

The most prominent, and certainly the most voluminous, writer of this time was undoubtedly Johann Mattheson, a man of universal accomplishments—well acquainted both with classical and modern languages, a fine organist and player on the harpsichord, composer, tenor singer, politician, and secretary of the English Legation at Hamburg. Every German of that time was pedantic, and Mattheson was no exception ; his books bubble over with amusing self-complacency, while in controversy he is rough-tongued and opinionated. But his knowledge was both solid and extensive.

The most famous of his didactic works is *Der Vollkommene Kapellmeister* (Hamburg, 1739 : folio), a handbook of all the acquirements which go to the formation of the perfect music-director. It contains much information on the various forms of musical composition then in vogue, which even now is of great interest. His *Exemplarische Organisten-Probe im Artikel vom General-Bass* (Hamburg,

1719: 4to ; with an excellent portrait of the author) consists of an elaborate treatise on the ratios of intervals and the science of harmony, followed by examples of figured basses, with explanations of the method of filling them up. A second and enlarged edition of this work was published as *Grosse General-Bass Schule* (Hamburg, 1731 : 4to), and an English translation exists. In 1735 he published a *Kleine General-Bass Schule* (Hamburg : 4to), not, as might be supposed, an abridgment of the previous book, but a perfectly distinct work, beginning with the more elementary stage of musical knowledge, and comprising some instructions for the harpsichord. His *Kern Melodisches Wissenschaft* (Hamburg, 1737 : 4to) goes over much of the ground traversed afterwards in the *Vollkommene Kapellmeister.*

There is a curious little book by Mattheson (if we may call a book little which, although small in size, contains at least seventeen hundred pages !) which may be spoken of under didactic works, although it is this and something more. Its title, or rather that of the first volume, which we transcribe in full, as it explains the purpose of the work and shows his ridiculous affectation in the use of three languages, is :—*Das Neu Eröffnete Orchestre,*

*oder Universelle und gründliche Anleitung
wie ein Galant Homme einen vollkomm-
nen Begriff von der Hoheit und Würde der
edlen Music erlangen, seinen Gout darnach
formiren, die Terminos technicos verstehen
und geschicklich von dieser vortrefflichen
Wissenschafft raisonniren möge* (Hamburg, 1713: 12mo). The second and
third volumes, under slightly varying titles,
appeared in 1717 and 1721. The object
of the book, as will have been seen from
the title, was to impart sufficient knowledge to the amateur to enable him to
take an intelligent interest in the music
which he heard.

In this volume the author had very
rightly accepted the addition of the
seventh degree of the scale, which had
already come into general use, forming
the diatonic scale, now universal, which
distinguishes the modern from the ancient
schools of composition.

But there were still those who clung to
the older tradition, and among these was
a musician of the name of Buttstett, a
man of some celebrity, both as an organist
and as a composer, who was induced to
launch a quarto volume of his belief, in
opposition to Mattheson. The title of
this work is, *Ut, Re, Mi, Fa, Sol, La,
Tota Musica et Harmonia Æterna* (Erfurt,

s. a., but 1717). Mattheson was the last man to allow such a challenge to pass, so that, unfortunately for his " *galant-homme*," the greater part of his second volume is devoted to a refutation, in no measured terms, of Buttstett's attempt to stop a development which was inevitable. Of course, Mattheson had the best of the argument, which at the same time was wholly out of place in a work of that nature. The third volume opens with an attempt to lay down sound principles of musical criticism, and then proceeds to consider the question whether the interval of a fourth is a consonance or a dissonance, with elaborate discussions on the opinions of other musicians on that point, which at that time was warmly contested.

It will have been gathered from the description of this work that the faculty of keeping to the point was not a prominent quality in our author. It must be admitted, also, that the intolerable pedantry, which he shared with most of his countrymen at that time, makes his works but dreary reading. They are too numerous to give even their titles here, but we must say a few words on the subject of his critical writings, which are valuable, both on account of his opinions and also as materials for musical history. The first of these is the *Critica Musica*, a monthly publication extending from 1722 to 1725, forming two volumes quarto (Hamburg), which is the earliest attempt at a musical journal. In it several treatises on Music are translated into German, criticisms on different works are given, together with such musical news as Mattheson was able to collect. The work expired in 1725, but a further attempt of a similar nature, with the title of *Der Musicalische Patriot*, was initiated in January 1728. It appears to have been a weekly publication, and to have expired with the forty-third number. Among the contents of this magazine is a " History of the Opera at Hamburg," with a very interesting catalogue of the works produced. His valuable contributions to musical biography will be noticed elsewhere. It may be interesting to mention that his contributions to musical literature alone extend to upwards of eight thousand pages, and that these form a part only of his writings.

The greatest of the German theorists of this time was Friedrich Wilhelm Marpurg. His first work, *Die Kunst das Klavier zu Spielen*, was published in 1750 (Berlin,

4to; second part 1751), under the pseudonym of *Der Kritische Musikus an der Spree*; but in subsequent editions, of which there were several, the author's name appears. It is a practical treatise on playing the harpsichord and on the art of accompaniment, and was followed in 1755 by the *Anleitung zum Clavier-spielen*, a work of a more advanced nature.

His great works, *Abhandlung von der Fuge* (Berlin, 1753: 4to), and the *Handbuch bey dem General-Basse und der Composition* (Berlin, 1757–8: 4to), are those on which his fame rests, and they have formed the foundation of the theoretical education of many generations of musicians, since their publication. The work on fugue was translated into French by the author himself (Berlin, 1756: 4to). His *Anleitung zur Sing-composition* (Berlin, 1758: 4to) is an admirable work on the art of setting words to music, with special reference to the prosody both of German, Italian, and Latin, while the mathematical calculation of musical intervals, and the question of Temperament, are considered in his *Anfangsgründe der Theoretischen Musik* (Berlin, 1757: 4to) and his *Anfangsgründe der progressional figurlichen Zifferkalkuls* (Berlin, 1774: 8vo).

Marpurg was equally distinguished in

the realms of criticism. His *Kritische Einleitung in die Geschichte und Lehrsätze der alten und neuen Musik* (Berlin, 1759 : 4to) is a history of ancient music in which much attention is given to the vexed question as to whether the Greeks practised harmony. He made three several attempts to found a journal of current criticism, the first under the title of *Der Critische Musicus an der Spree* (Berlin : 4to), which appeared weekly from March 4th, 1749, to February 17th, 1750. It may be well to remind the reader that the Spree is the name of the sluggish river on which Berlin is situated. Complete sets of this publication are of very unusual occurrence. His next attempt, *Historisch-Kritische Beytrage zur Aufnahme der Musik* (Berlin, 1754–62 : forming 5 vols., 8vo), had a longer existence, but it is remarkable that during its currency he started a third serial, the *Kritische Briefe über die Tonkunst* (Berlin, 1759–64 : 4to), also published weekly. The letters were frequently addressed to distinguished musicians, but this probably was merely a literary artifice. There can be no doubt that Marpurg was also the author of a little book—*Legende einiger Musikheiligen* (Cologne, 1786 : 8vo) —purporting to be by "Simeon Metaphrastes the younger," which is a collection of anecdotes about Music and musicians.

The fame of Kirnberger as a theorist was scarcely inferior to that of Marpurg. His most important publication was *Die Kunst des reinen Satzes in der Musik* (Berlin : 2 vols., 4to; the first without date, the second, which is chiefly devoted to double counterpoint, in 1777). Kirnberger was a pupil of J. S. Bach, and it is to be regretted that he published no treatise on the art of fugue, embodying the practice of his immortal master. No doubt a long illness, terminated by his premature death, prevented such an undertaking.

Although an Austrian, and not a German, the name of Fux is so often connected with those of Marpurg and Kirnberger that we may be allowed to speak here of his famous *Gradus ad Parnassum*, a title amply justified by the results of its teaching. The first edition, in Latin, appeared at Vienna in 1725, in an admirably printed folio volume, with a finely engraved frontispiece, under the auspices of his consistent patron the Emperor Charles VI., who bore the cost of its publication. The work is a lucid and well-arranged exposition of the rules of musical composition in all the various styles, partly carried on in the form of a dialogue between master and pupil. Its merit was at once recognised and it was translated into all the principal languages of Europe. The three writers, Fux, Marpurg, and Kirnberger, were for years looked on as the court of appeal in all questions of musical orthodoxy.

The name of Georg Andreas Sorge also stands high as a musical theorist; his principal work is *Vorgemach der musikalischen Composition* (Lohenstein, 1745-7 : 4to), the professed aim of which is, in the words of the title, to render the "*Studiosus Musices*" a "*Compositor extemporaneus.*" But he was also favourably known for his researches into the scientific principles of Music, and especially into the question of Temperament.

There was no want of lesser lights in the musical firmament to aid in dissipating the darkness of ignorance. These were frequently men of great learning, who devoted themselves to the task of imparting it with true German thoroughness. Among the foremost of these must be mentioned Joseph Riepel, who published an *Anfangsgründe zur Musikalischen Setzkunst* (Augsburg, 1752 : folio). The complete work consists of six parts, the last of which was published at Ratisbon in

1786, the whole forming a formidable volume which probably no one in the present day has read ; perhaps in an earlier generation some student, as earnest as the author, may have made the study of it the work of his life.   The *Tractatus Musicus Compositorio-Practicus, Das ist, Musikalischer Tractat* of the learned Benedictine Meinardus Spiess (Augsburg, 1746 : folio) professes to be written in German, but it is so interlarded with Latin that the well-known musician J. A. Hiller proposed that it should be translated from German into German.

As we have previously said, nearly all the German works of this period are distinguished by a strange jumble of languages in their titles.   A book intended for self-instruction by J. P. Eisel (although his name does not appear) carries off the palm for what we suppose must have been considered a merit at that time.   He contrives to use four languages in the first six lines of the title, as follows :—
Musicus αυτοδίδακτος, *oder Der sich selbst informirende Musicus bestehend sowohl in Vocal-als üblicher Instrumental-Musique,* (Erfurt, 1738 : 4to).   The book, which is written in the form of question and answer, is not without interest, for among other information it describes the various in-

struments then in use, with diagrams of
the fingering of the different wind instruments. Facing page 70 is a very quaint
cut of a gentleman playing the musical
glasses.

In Italy Padre Martini was the living
representative of the traditions of the
great Roman School. His historical
labours will be noticed elsewhere, but
we must in this place mention his *Exem-
plare o sia Saggio Fundamentale pratico di
Contrappunto sopra il Canto Fermo*,
(Bologna, 1774 : 2 vols., 4to), the second
volume being devoted to contrappunto
fugato. The work is throughout based
on the tonality of the ancient Plain-Song,
and the plan of it consists in selecting
passages from the great writers of the
Roman and Spanish Schools, with a
running commentary of great learning and
value on the musical treatment of the
different compositions. The plan had
already been adopted with success by his
pupil Giuseppe Paolucci in his *Arte
pratica di Contrappunto* (Venice, 1765,
1766, 1772 : 3 vols., 4to). Both works are
exceedingly valuable, not only for their
admirable exposition of the principles of
the greatest school of sacred vocal writing,
but also for the interest of the musical
examples, many of which are not readily

to be met with in a separate form. The whole of the examples chosen by Martini were subsequently included by Choron in his *Principes de Composition des Écoles d'Italie* (Paris, 1808 : 3 vols., folio).

A book which excited much attention at this time, and fluttered the dovecotes of the orthodox musicians, was entitled *Dell' origine e delle Regole della Musica, colla storia del suo progresso, decadenza e rinnovazione* (Rome, 1774 : 4to) by a learned Spanish Jesuit, D. Antonio Eximeno, who had been long established in Italy. The work was a revolt against the trammels of the strict laws of counterpoint. The author approached Music from the æsthetic side alone, maintaining that its primary intention is to express emotion. The theorists were up in arms, and even the placid temper of Padre Martini gave way. Eximeno replied in a *Dubbio di D. Antonio Eximeno sopra il Saggio Fundamentale pratico di Contrappunto del R. P. Maestro Giambattista Martini* (Rome, 1775 : 4to). The controversy coincided with the gradual extinction of the noble school of composition in Italy.

In France the most prominent figure was undoubtedly Jean Philippe Rameau, the inventor of the system of the " Fundamental Bass "—a discovery which his contemporary admirers did not hesitate to compare to those of Newton. His first theoretical work, the *Traité de l'Harmonie réduite à ses Principes naturels* was published in Paris in 1722 (4to), and in it is the first enunciation of the theory. It seems remarkable that the law of inversion in chords, from which the system of fundamental bass is derived, should have remained undiscovered until so late a period in musical history. The research and industry of Rameau is borne witness to by the works which he published in further development of his system. In 1726 appeared his *Nouveau système de Musique Théorique . . . pour servir d'Introduction au Traité de l'Harmonie* (Paris : 4to), in 1737 his *Génération harmonique, ou Traité de Musique Théorique et Pratique* (Paris : 8vo), and in 1760 the *Code de Musique Pratique* (Paris : 4to), and during this time a succession of pamphlets of a controversial nature in defence of different points of his theories ; and all these works were written during the constant occupation of composing and producing new operas. It must be admitted that the style of Rameau is greatly wanting in clearness, so that some resolution is called for in reading his works.

This deficiency of the author was felt by his friend, D'Alembert, who produced, anonymously, *Élémens de Musique, théorique et pratique suivant les Principes de M. Rameau* (Paris, 1759: 8vo), with a view of placing his views before the public in a smaller compass, and in more intelligible language.

The theories of Rameau almost at once received a wide acceptation. They led Marpurg to modify his views. In France their warmest advocate was the Abbé Roussier, who published a *Traité des Accords et de leur Succession, selon le Système de la Basse Fondamentale* (Paris, 1764 : 8vo), and the more important parts of the *Traité de l'Harmonie* was within a few years translated into English.

It was a legitimate object of ambition with Rameau to be entrusted with the articles on Music in the famous *Encyclopédie* of Diderot and D'Alembert, but in this he was disappointed, and the work was given to J. J. Rousseau, who possessed few of the qualifications for such an undertaking, as the result proved. Rameau was not slow to seize on the opportunity, by publishing his *Erreurs sur la Musique dans l'Encyclopédie* (Paris, 1755: 8vo). Rousseau wrote a reply, which was only published after his death, in the collection of his works. He was gradually led to acknowledge the justice of these strictures, and entered on a course of deeper study, which resulted in his famous *Dictionary*, of which we shall have to speak later, as also of his contributions to the *Guerre des Bouffons.*

It can hardly be necessary to speak of Ballière, Jamard, Mercadier de Belesta, and other French theorists, whose works have now an interest only for the student of the development of the science of Harmony. Such persons I would refer to the *Esquisse de l'Historie de l'Harmonie* of the late M. Fétis (Paris, 1840 : 8vo), a little work of very great interest, reprinted from the *Gazette Musicale* as presents for the author's friends, which, in consequence, is unfortunately of exceeding rarity.

There is one writer, however, who must be mentioned here, as the student of musical literature is sure to run against some of his works very early in his course. This is Bémetzrieder, whose principal claim to celebrity is his charlatanry. An Alsatian and an ex-Benedictine, he found his way to Paris, ready to turn to account any of the various accomplishments to which he laid claim. On the advice of Diderot he adopted Music as the readiest means of livelihood, the philosopher's daughter becoming his first pupil. For her he wrote his well-known *Leçons de Clavecin et Principes d'Harmonie* (Paris, 1771 : 4to), which owes its literary shape entirely to Diderot. The book is in the form of a dialogue between master and pupil, and is certainly amusing; it obtained for Bémetzrieder great vogue as a teacher among the upper classes. Many other works succeeded it, but it seems that he soon dropped out of fashion, for in 1782 he settled in London, where he brought out several works.

In England it must be admitted that musical literature languished during the earlier part of the eighteenth century. The first work that claims notice is Alexander Malcolm's *Treatise of Musick, Speculative, Practical, and Historical* (Edinburgh, 1721 : 8vo). The book covers the whole field of musical knowledge, and the author has the gift of clear exposition. The portion on tuning and Temperament is excellent.

Among the many schemes for simplifying musical notation was the *New System of Music, both Theorical and Practical, And yet not Mathematical*, by James Francis De La Fond, a Frenchman, settled in England, where he became a teacher of languages and Music. His grievance with the existing notation was that a degree of the stave did not always represent the same interval; for example, in the key of C, from C to D, and from D to E—*i.e.*, from the third space in the treble to the fourth line, and from the fourth line to the fourth space, each represent a whole tone, while from the fourth space to the fifth line (from E to F) is only a semitone; and he overcame this by dividing the octave into twelve semitones, each of which was distinguished by a line or a space. The author was a man of original views on most points, among others on spelling, and he frequently breaks off from his main argument to defend his opinions; he looked on "samifying" as a better word than "identifying" —but then, he was a "Foreiner." It is to be supposed that the book met with but little success, for it concludes with the words "End of the first volume," but no continuation is known to have existed.

The popularity of the little handbooks of Playford and Sympson continued well on into this century; it was partly shared by the *Modern Music Master, or the Universal Musician* of Peter Prelleur, also a Frenchman (London, 1730: 8vo).

In 1730 appeared anonymously *A Short Treatise on Harmony.* It was supposed

to be by Lord Paisley, afterwards Earl of
Abercorn, but it consisted simply of the
rules which Dr. Pepusch had written for
his use, without the examples necessary to
explain them. Dr. Pepusch was naturally
annoyed that his work should be produced in such a shape, so that in self-
defence he brought out a second edition
(London, 1731 : obl. 4to), still, however,
without appending his name as author.
In 1737 John Frederick Lampe, also a
German, settled in England, published his
*Plain and Compendious Method of teaching
Thorough Bass* (London : 4to), which he
followed up in 1740 with his *Art of
Musick* (London : 8vo), in both of which
he shows himself a disciple of Rameau.
And in 1770 John Holden, a professor
of Music in Glasgow, produced *An Essay
towards a rational system of Music*
(Glasgow : obl. 4to), also strongly imbued
with the principles of Rameau, in which
the whole science of Music is explained
with great method and clearness.

A book which attracted much attention
in the musical world was published by
Charles Avison, organist of Newcastle-on-
Tyne, with the title *An Essay on Musical
Expression* (London, 1752 : 8vo). In it
the author freely delivers his opinions on
the comparative merits of the various com-

posers in vogue. It was these judgments which brought the book into notice. He was without doubt a scholar and a man of some literary taste, but we cannot greatly respect the soundness of his critical faculties when they lead him to exalt Marcello and Geminiani at the expense of a master of such surpassing powers as Handel. We are far from underrating the works of Marcello, and his admirers owe a debt of gratitude to Avison for the assistance and support given to John Garth, organist of Durham, in the production of the only English edition of that admirable musician's Psalms, now, alas ! almost forgotten ; but to compare Geminiani, a merely elegant composer, with Marcello, and to place the two on a higher pinnacle than the giant Handel, shows a twist of intellect, and a want of sense of proportion, which is inexplicable. It was not long before Dr. W. Hayes, then Professor of Music at the University of Oxford, joined issue in his *Remarks on Mr. Avison's Essay on Musical Expression* (London, 1753 : 8vo), and in the same year Avison issued a second edition of his *Essay*, with the addition of an Appendix, in reply, towards which he is said to have had the assistance of Dr. Jortin, who also added a letter to the author, concerning the music of the Ancients.

This brings us to the latter years of the eighteenth century, which were destined to be the period of the greatest glory of musical literature in this country, for in it were written those two great histories of Music by Burney and Hawkins which have formed the foundation of nearly all that has been since written on the subject. These will be considered in our next chapter, but we may here notice the interesting travels of Dr. Burney in search of materials for his great undertaking. *The Present State of Music in France and Italy* appeared in 1771 (London : 8vo). Among much that is interesting there is an account of an interview with the famous Padre Martini, who was himself at that time engaged on a similar work. This volume was followed by two others on *The Present State of Music in Germany, the Netherlands, and the United Provinces.* This work, published in 1773, recounts his relations with Metastasio (whose life he afterwards wrote), Hasse and Gluck. It is worthy of note that the excellent Abbot Gerbert, who also formed a friendship with Martini, had published an account of his travels in search of materials for his famous *Scriptores*, under the title of *Iter Alemannicum, accedit Italicum et Gallicum* (Saint Blaise, 1765 : 8vo) which may have suggested the publication of these works to Burney.

It is not surprising that the ardent satisfaction with which Burney records the politeness of his reception by the different persons of eminence to whom he bore letters of introduction should have formed the ground for some good-humoured banter. This found vent in *Musical Travels through England*, by Joel Collier, Licentiate in Music (London, 1774 : 8vo)—perhaps a little too free for present tastes—said to have been written by a musician named J. L. Bicknell. Fétis asserts that Burney and Bicknell bought up the copies, and that it is consequently rare ; but both the fact and the supposed result seem doubtful.

CHAPTER VI.

Histories of Music—Biography.

AVING traced the principal objects with which musical literature occupied itself in the different countries of Europe to the end of the eighteenth century, we now propose to consider some of the special branches into which it has been directed. Among these the history of Music undoubtedly holds the first place. Much historical information is, of course, to be found in many of the works already noticed, but we are now about to speak of those which are professedly historical.

The first serious attempt at a general history of Music was Printz's *Historische Beschreibung der Edelen Sing und Kling-Kunst* (Dresden, 1690 : 4to). The earlier part of the work, containing the history of Music among the ancients, is superseded by the more accurate scholarship of the present day, but in its information about the musicians who immediately preceded the author, or were his contemporaries, it is one of the most valuable sources of information.

The *Historia Musica* of G. A. Angelini Bontempi (Perugia, 1695 : folio) is a little disappointing, for it actually consists of dissertations on the ancient and modern theory and practice of Music, and in no respect justifies its title.

The earliest attempt at a history of Music in France was by Jacques Bonnet, and a very feeble attempt it was. The materials were collected by the Abbé Bourdelot (who, in spite of his title, was a physician and not an ecclesiastic) and they were arranged and published after his death by Bonnet, who was his nephew. The first edition appeared under the title of *Histoire de la Musique et de ses effets* (Paris, 1715 : 12mo). Bonnet's name does not appear on the title, but is appended to the dedication, and in the preface he duly acknowledges his indebtedness to his uncle, and to his brother Pierre Bonnet, to whom his uncle had left his papers, on condition that he took the name of Bourdelot and completed the History. Pierre's death prevented this, and the work passed to his younger brother Jacques. The book went through more editions than its merits warranted ; the last has the

Hague and Frankfurt on the title and is dated 1743. Bourdelot's name appears as author in all editions after the first, and the work is extended to four duodecimo volumes. Of these the first alone contains the work of Bonnet—or Bourdelot ; the other three consist of a reprint, under Bourdelot's name, of the *Comparaison de la Musique italienne et de la Musique française* of *Le Cerf de la Viéville.* It is in each case a Dutch printer to whom this discreditable act is due. Jacques Bonnet was somewhat crack-brained, and it is on the authority of this History alone that the well-known and romantic story of Stradella rests. The *Histoire générale, critique et philologique de la Musique* of Blainville (Paris, 1767 : 4to) is of the very smallest value.

It was not till 1757 that a history of Music on an adequate scale, by a writer possessing the necessary qualifications, began to see the light. In that year the learned and famous Padre Giambatista Martini published the first volume of his *Storia della Musica,* which at once placed him in the front rank of writers on Music. Martini was fifty-one years of age when this volume appeared, which was succeeded in 1770 and 1781 by the second and third volumes (Bologna : 4to). The three

volumes bring this history down to no
later a date than the Greeks. A fourth
volume was to have treated of the music
of the Middle Ages, but this, alas ! the
learned father did not live to complete.
It was supposed that the MS. was ready
for the press, but the researches of Fétis
proved that only a few materials existed.
The book thus remains a magnificent fragment, containing, on the period covered, all
the information that was available at the
time of its publication. The work is so
ample in its treatment, and so brimful of
learning and research, that it is impossible
to conceive how many volumes would have
been necessary to bring it down to modern
times ; and one is tempted to regret the
vastness of scale which rendered its completion by the labours of a single man
impossible.

Each chapter begins and ends with a
puzzle canon, resolutions of the whole of
which were published by Cherubini. The
book is excellently printed and illustrated,
and is by no means uncommon. A copy
is occasionally met with, sumptuously
printed in large folio, with ornamental
borders, the text being identical. These
were designed by the Padre as presents
for Sovereigns and other great personages.

A few years after the appearance of

Martini's second volume, two other works of the first importance burst upon the world, and both in our own country. In 1776 the first volume of Dr. Burney's *History* appeared ; about four months later the five volumes of Sir John Hawkins' *History* were published together (London, 1776 : 4to). Dr. Burney's work was completed in four volumes quarto, the second appearing in 1781, and the concluding volumes in 1789. They are both works of which a nation may be proud, and both fortunate in that the authors were enabled to carry out to completion the plan they had laid down for themselves. It is curious that two men, one a learned professor, the other a well-qualified amateur, and both of them members of THE Club, should have undertaken so extensive a work, bounded by the same limits, at the same time, and entirely independently.

In comparing the two works critically, it must be admitted that "that clever dog Burney," as Dr. Johnson was fond of calling him, was well equipped for the undertaking. In addition to adequate training as a musician he was an excellent scholar, and possessed the art of writing with skill and taste. On theoretical subjects he speaks, of course, with greater authority than Sir J. Hawkins. It is to be regretted that his admiration for the works of foreign composers led him to undervalue those of Englishmen. His account of our great school of madrigal writers is meagre to the last degree, showing that his acquaintance with a period which forms one of the chief glories of the English school was of the slightest; while his unconcealed contempt for those he vouchsafes to mention does little credit to his critical faculties. With the style of Purcell he had greater sympathy, so that of him his notice is more appreciative. With Handel he was personally acquainted, and the account he gives of the earlier part of his life in this country, and of his operatic career, is both detailed and interesting, forming one of the chief sources of information for the particulars of this portion of the composer's career. The account of his oratorios is disappointing.

There is no doubt that contemporary opinion was entirely in favour of Dr. Burney; and indeed, it was a bold attempt on the part of an amateur to undertake so formidable a work as a history of Music, and to publish it in its completeness in five quarto volumes, knowing that a professional musician of eminence was engaged in a like task. The fact proves that he was in no way indebted to the researches of his professional rival. The result fully justified the boldness of the attempt. The style is not so polished, and the work possibly not such amusing reading as that of his rival, but in research and accuracy it need fear no comparison. A large number of well-selected examples add greatly to its value, and many portraits of musicians are given—those of English musicians principally copied from the paintings in the Oxford Music School. Not having enjoyed the advantage of foreign travel, the author was under no obligation to decry that which was English, and his account of the works of our own madrigalists is both adequate and appreciative. Sir John Hawkins must have been a man of very remarkable powers and attainments; there can be little doubt that Boswell looked on him with jealousy—probably for the reason that Johnson made him one of his executors—for the biographer never mentions him in the *Life* except in terms of depreciation.

Contemporary opinion has been reversed. Burney has never been reprinted, while Hawkins has been issued in a convenient form, with notes which more recent knowledge has rendered necessary, by Messrs. Novello & Co. ; in this form it is still obtainable, and will be found most useful.

The next serious attempt at a history based on original research was that of Johann Nicholaus Forkel, an esteemed critic and writer on Music. The first volume of his *Allgemeine Geschichte der Musik* appeared in 1788 (Leipzig: 4to), the second not until 1801. The writer had the advantage of the previous labours of Martini, Burney, and Hawkins, and rightly made use of them ; but he was very painstaking and accurate—indeed, much too minute in detail, treating important and unimportant points with the same exhaustiveness, so that the subject proceeds with somewhat irritating deliberation. The second volume carries us no further than the middle of the sixteenth century. The author died in 1818, not having completed the third volume, for which he had collected a large mass of materials. These were offered to Choron and to Fétis, with the view of their completing the work. Many difficulties prevented the adoption of this scheme, and the work remains a fragment, useful principally as a storehouse of facts, in the main trustworthy.

One of the reasons which induced Fétis

to decline the proposal was that he had already conceived the plan of a work, on lines altogether different from those followed by Forkel. It resulted in the masterly *Résumé philosophique de l'Histoire de la Musique*, which forms the introduction to the first edition of his *Biographie universelle des Musiciens* (Brussels, 1837–44 : 8 vols., 8vo). It fully carries out its title, and in two hundred and eighteen octavo pages gives an admirably succinct and well-arranged account of the gradual development of the art of Music, certainly far in advance of anything existing up to that time. It is to be regretted that, not being published in separate form, it is not obtainable apart from the rest of the work, now wholly superseded by a later edition to which this *Résumé* is not appended, for the reason that Fétis had decided on writing an independent history of Music. Like so many attempts of this nature, the undertaking was never completed : two volumes appeared during the life of the author (Paris, 1869 : 8vo) ; the third was passing through the press when death put a stop to a career of bewildering activity, the day after he had completed his eighty-seventh year. Three more volumes were ready for the press, and they were produced under the supervision of the author's son, in 1874-76. In this work the author treats the subject in his usual magisterial style. On every point his opinion is stated with unerring clearness and conviction, from which no appeal is permissible ; nor was he the man to give other writers the credit of the views which he had done them the honour to adopt. There can be no doubt that he was largely indebted for many of his facts to La Fage, of whom, however, he always speaks with depreciation ; and the illustrations of Assyrian musical instruments, and in many cases the descriptions of them, have been taken from C. Engel's *Music of the most ancient Nations*, without any acknowledgment.

It is a little curious that, having found himself unable to continue the work of Forkel, his own labours should have come to a termination at the same period—the fifteenth century. Great advance has been made in the study of ethnology during the present century, so that Fétis stands on much firmer ground than his predecessors when treating of the musical efforts—in many cases rude enough—of various nations possessing but an imperfect civilisation. He insists, with great success, on the universality of the pentatonic scale among such peoples. The music of the Hebrews and of the Greeks is treated at great length, but one cannot help a feeling of regret that the author was not content to pass much of this by, and to give us a history of that *Art* of Music, as practised by the civilised world, which forms our great inheritance.

We have just mentioned the name of Adrien de La Fage. His *Histoire générale de la Musique et de la Danse* (Paris, 1844 : 2 vols., 8vo) adds one more to the list of works on the subject which were destined to remain uncompleted. The two volumes published treat of the music of China, India, Egypt, and of the Hebrews, and it may be well to mention that they should be accompanied by a folio volume of examples and illustrations, which is frequently wanting. La Fage was a man of great learning, and the *Histoire* is an excellent work as far as it goes ; probably it did not receive sufficient support to warrant its continuance.

For the last of the great attempts at a history of Music we are indebted to a German—originally, and till his fiftieth year, a hard-worked official in the Austrian Civil Service—who, strange to say, in his youth was taught every accomplishment *except* Music, which, it was feared, would

unfit him for the career for which he was
destined. This remarkable man was
August Wilhelm Ambros. Having made
himself favourably known by several essays
in musical criticism, he produced the
first volume of his *Geschichte der Musik*
in 1862, the successive volumes appearing
in 1864, 1868, 1878 (Leipzig: 8vo), the
last a fragment, edited after the death of
the author by his friend E. Schelle. This
is one of the most important and authoritative books of our own time, and is characterised by careful investigation, great
learning, sound judgment, and, what is
perhaps rarer among German writers, by
an agreeable style. The first volume
treats of the music of China, India, Arabia,
and Greece. Vol. ii. is occupied with
early Christian music, Gregorian Plain-
Song, Hucbald, Guido d'Arezzo, the
Troubadours and Minnesingers, and the
origin of harmony. Vol. iii. introduces
us to the great school of the Netherlands,
and traces its wide-spread influence over
the rest of Europe. Our early English
musicians are not overlooked. We are
then carried to Venice, and the volume
concludes with an account of the predecessors of Palestrina in Rome and the
south of Italy. Vol. iv. begins with the
great period of the Roman School—that

of Palestrina and his disciples—and then proceeds to the consideration of the rise of the Opera in Italy under Caccini and Peri, and of the innovations of Monteverde. Some space is given to the theorists of that time—Zarlino, Zacconi, Artusi, and others; and a notice of the early organists—among whom are Banchieri, Frescobaldi and Froberger—brings this volume to a premature conclusion, which cannot be too deeply regretted, for in many respects it is the most valuable history which has appeared. A continuation, however, bringing the work down to recent times, has been brought out by Dr. Wilhelm Langhans (Leipzig, 1884, 1887: 2 vols., 8vo), the able Professor of Musical History at the Conservatoire of Berlin. A new edition of Ambros's work has lately been published, and if any one could be found enterprising enough to give an English translation of it, it would be a boon to many students.

These works are the most important of the histories which were designed to embrace the whole scope of the subject, and have formed the hunting ground of all subsequent writers. It will have been remarked that our own historians, Burney and Hawkins, are the only writers who have brought their labours to a termination, but this termination has now been left in the far-away past. To the professed student these works are a necessity, but the general reader will be glad of a book on a less extended scale, bringing our knowledge down to a more recent date. Of such works there is an abundance. Among the best known of these, and already long superannuated, is Dr. Busby's *General History of Music* (London, 1829 : 2 vols., 8vo), which is little more than a compilation from Burney and Hawkins. The *History of Music*, by W. C. Stafford (Edinburgh, 1830: 12mo) formed a volume of Constable's *Miscellany*, and received the unmerited honour of translation, both into French (by Madame Fétis) and into German. In 1834 George Hogarth, the well-known musical critic, published his *Musical History, Biography, and Criticism* (London: 12mo), an enlarged edition of which appeared in 1838. All these, however, have become somewhat "ancient history," and the reader will inquire for a work coming down to later times. Such is the *History of Music in the form of Lectures*, by F. L. Ritter, a native of Strasburg settled in America, where the work was originally published, but it has been reprinted more than once in this country;

or *A General History of Music,* by W. S. Rockstro (London, 1886: 8vo). They are both excellent works in a moderate compass. The late Sir G. A. Macfarren, also, reprinted his article on the history of Music from the last edition of the *Encyclopædia Britannica,* which is furnished with a useful " Roll " of the names of musicians, giving the places and dates of their births and deaths. The little *History of Music* by the Rev. J. Bonavia Hunt, Mus. Doc., has the merit of remarkable succinctness—perhaps somewhat at the expense of interest—and has become very popular as a textbook.

In Germany the most popular History appears to have been Dr. K. F. Brendel's *Geschichte der Musik in Italiens, Frankreich und Deutschland* (Leipzig, 1852: 8vo), which has been several times reprinted. Brendel had identified himself with the advanced school of German musicians, which no doubt has had influence on the popularity of the work—it cannot have been owing to the graces of its style. Another excellent history is the *Allgemeine Geschichte der Musik* of the very industrious and well-informed writer August Reissmann (Munich, 1863, 1864 3 vols. 8vo), a carefully planned work abounding in well-chosen examples. Both these are characterised by sound learning. Of a more popular nature is Dr. Emil Naumann's *Illustrirte Musik Geschichte* (Berlin, 1880–85 : 2 vols., 8vo), a work profusely illustrated with portraits and other woodcuts, but noticeable also for the numerous facsimiles of autograph compositions by the great composers, which recent developments of photography have rendered possible at a moderate outlay. The work has been translated into English by Ferdinand Præger, and was published in serial numbers by Messrs. Cassell & Co., having the advantage of the editorship of the late Rev. Sir F. A. Gore-Ouseley, who added some information on Music in this country.

The French have always excelled in the compilation of attractive popular works. Among these Félix Clément's *Histoire de la Musique* (Paris, 1885 : 8vo) must be noticed. It is a portly volume of eight hundred pages, freely illustrated. The writer is a man of wide acquirements, who has done much useful work in other departments of musical literature, and the History is distinguished by French clearness of statement and good arrangement. The *Histoire de la Musique* of H. Lavoix *fils* (Paris, *s.a.* [1884] : 8vo), on a smaller scale, is also well illustrated, and contains many facsimiles of the autographs of musicians.

Among the most useful works of original research on musical history will be found those numerous monographs which confine themselves to the history of a particular country, or to that of a particular department or period. Prominent among the latter stands the name of Raphael Georg Kiesewetter. His earliest appearance as a writer on Music was in his prize essay on the influence of the musicians of the Netherlands on the musical schools of Italy—*Verhandelingen over de Vraag : welke verdiensten hebben zich de Nederlanders vooral in de* 14ᵉ, 15ᵉ, *en* 16ᵉ *eeuw in het vak der Toonkunst vorworven* (Amsterdam, 1829 : 4to). The work is in German, the title only in Dutch. To this essay the gold medal of the Netherlands Institute was awarded, while Fétis received the silver medal. The two works were printed together, and both are distinguished by masterly treatment of a subject of the highest interest in musical history. His next work was the *Geschichte der europäisch-abendländischen oder unser heutigen Musik* (Leipzig, 1834 : 4to ; 2nd edition, *ib.*, 1846), of which an English translation by R. Müller, under the title of *History of the Modern Music of Western Europe*, appeared (London, 1848: 8vo). The most valuable part of this work is undoubtedly the history of the earlier periods; with modern music the writer had but little sympathy, and it is dismissed in a very few pages. He next gave to the world his treatise, *Ueber die Musik der neueren Griechen, nebst freien Gedanken über altegyptische und altgriechische Musik* (Leipzig, 1838 : 4to), in which he joins issue with some of the opinions expressed by Fétis in his *Résumé philosophique.* The last work of Kiesewetter which we shall mention is his *Schicksale und Beschaffenheit des weltlichen Gesanges* (Leipzig, 1841 : 4to), which contains the results of much research into the early history of the Opera.

In England perhaps the most remarkable modern publication has been the late Mr. William Chappell's *History of Music* (London, 1874 : 8vo), a work which, with the assistance of other writers, was to have been completed in four volumes. The first only was published; a few sheets of the second volume were in type, when a fire at the printing office destroyed them, and the author, already an old man, does not seem to have had the heart to go over his labour a second time. Not that the single volume published shows any want of energy ! On the contrary, it is characterised throughout by a most remarkable spirit of pugnacity. Almost all the accepted authorities, from Boethius to Helmholtz, come in for a castigation. The author claims to have placed our knowledge of Grecian music on a firm basis, to have established the existence of simultaneous harmony among the ancients, and to have explained the hydraulic organ of Vitruvius. The volume is mainly occupied with the music of the Greeks, and, whether agreeing or not with its conclusion, the reader cannot fail to be delighted with its really youthful vigour.

Of a less exhilarating nature, but truly excellent books, are the two courses of lectures by the late John Hullah, republished under the titles of *The History of Modern Music* (London, 1861 : 8vo ; 2nd edition, 1875), and *The Transition Period of Musical History* (London, 1865 : 8vo; 2nd edition, 1876). The former covers the period from A.D. 370 to our own time, while the *Transition* treats with greater detail of the period from 1600 to 1750, covering the rise of our modern music from the time of Monteverde. The writer was a thoroughly capable and accomplished musician, and both works are most useful and to be recommended. The *Transition* contains a number of interesting examples, while the *Modern History* is furnished with a series of chronological tables, in the form of diagrams, showing what musicians were contemporary, on a principle first used (in musical history, at least) by Dr. Crotch in his printed lectures.

It is difficult to know how to speak of Mr. J. F. Rowbotham's *History of Music* (London, 1885, 1886, 1887 : 3 vols., 8vo). The work is complete according to the author's intentions, but it carries us no further than the Troubadours, so that the title is somewhat misleading. The earlier part of the work exhibits a profound acquaintance with ethnological literature as far as it concerns Music, and the leading idea is that from the dawn of civilisation Music has gradually developed through the Drum stage, the Pipe stage, and the Lyre stage, and this theory is supported with great wealth of illustration. The Lyre stage appears not to have been reached till the time of the Egyptians, whose music and instruments, as well as those of the Assyrians and Hebrews, are considered at some length. The music of the Chinese and Hindus is next treated

of, while vol. ii. is almost entirely devoted to the music of the Greeks, an
elaborate investigation of the various
rhythms and metres occupying the largest
share of the space.   Vol. iii. opens with the
" Decline of Paganism, and the dark Ages,"
containing the history of the adoption of
the Church Modes, with much information
on early systems of musical notation, and
an elaborate description of the " neums."
The remainder of the volume traces the
history of Music during the Middle Ages,
the supposed influence of Arabian music,
concluding with an account of the Troubadours.   It is a bewildering book, beginning with the history of Music among
pre-historic nations, of which we con-
fessedly know nothing, and terminating
on what is almost the threshold of the
subject.   There is no index—not even any
headings to the chapters—while the display of learning becomes oppressive and
the style wearisome.

An excellent work, going over much of
the same ground, is the *Primitive Music :
an inquiry into the origin and development of Music, Song, Intruments, Dances,
and Pantomime of Savage Races,* by
Richard Wallaschek (London, 1893 : 8vo),
which owes its English form to Mr.
R. H. Legge.

The works on the history of the music of particular nations form a large class, a few only of which can be named here. Among the most important is the *Historia de la Musica Española* of Mariano Soriano Fuertes (Madrid, 1855-9 : 4 vols., 8vo)—an excellent work, devoted to Music in Spain, containing information not otherwise attainable. For the history of Music in Germany the only one requiring notice is Reissmann's *Illustrirte Geschichte* (Leipzig, 1881 : 8vo), a well-illustrated work, with some excellent facsimiles. That of France is represented by Poisot's *Histoire de la Musique en France* (Paris, 1860 : 12mo) ; the same writer also produced an *Essai sur les Musiciens bourguignons* (Dijon, 1854 : 8vo), while M. Albert Jacquot brought out a sumptuous volume, *La Musique en Lorraine* (Paris, 1882 : 8vo). Music in England has received but scant attention : *The Old Cheque-Book of the Chapel Royal from* 1561 *to* 1744, edited by the late Dr. Rimbault for the Camden Society (1872 : 4to), and the *Memoirs of Musick* of the Hon. Roger North, written in 1728, but published for the first time in 1846, (London : 4to), also under the auspices of Dr. Rimbault, are rather materials towards it than actual history, although of very great value. The only historical work devoted exclusively to England with which we are acquainted is Dr. F. L. Ritter's *Music in England*, the original American edition of which the writer has not seen ; but it was reprinted in London in 1884, octavo, with a companion volume on Music in America. It will be well, perhaps, to mention here Mr. W. A. Barrett's little work on *English Glee Writers* (London, 1886 : 8vo), an excellent *résumé* of a notable period of our musical history.

Several good local histories exist of Italian music. Of these we must mention Villarosa's *Memorie dei Compositori di Musica di Napoli* (Naples, 1840: 8vo) and Florimo's *La Scuola Musicale di Napoli*, of which two editions have appeared, the first, Naples, 1869, 1871 : 2 vols., 8vo ; the second, *ib.*, 1881 : 4 vols., 8vo, a carefully executed work. Alessandro Sala brought out *I musicisti Veronesi* (Verona, 1879 : 8vo), and G. Gaspari, *La Musica in Bologna* (Bologna, *s.a.* : 8vo). No Italian book exists, as far as we know, embracing the general history of Music in that country. A Russian, Count Orloff, attempted an *Essai sur l'Histoire de la Musique en Italie* (Paris, 1822 : 2 vols., 8vo)—a wretched compilation, full of errors in the spelling of proper names, which seem to have proceeded from ignorance rather than carelessness. In spite of its worthlessness it was translated both into German and into Italian. A much better work is E. Naumann's *Die Italienischen Tondichter* (Berlin, 1876 : 8vo).

Of special works on the music of Oriental nations, we must add to those already mentioned on that of the Hebrews, Salomon Van Til's *Digt-, Sang- en Speel-Konst, soo der Ouden, als bysonder der Hebreen* (Dordrecht, 1692 : 4to), several Dutch editions of which exist, while two editions were printed of the German translation (Frankfurt and Leipzig, 1706 and 1719: 4to). Arabian music has come in for much attention. In addition to the work of Kiesewetter on the subject, *Die Musik der Araber* (Leipzig, 1842 : 4to), we have the *Esquisse Historique de la Musique Arabe* by Christianowitsch (Cologne, 1863 : 4to) a somewhat sketchy performance, and *La Musique Arabe, ses rapports avec la Musique Greeque et la Chant Grégorien* of Salvador Daniel (Algiers, 1863 : 8vo), the almost unknown musician who, on the death of Auber, was appointed by the Commune Principal of the Conservatoire at Paris. On the entry of the regular troops into the city he was seized while firing upon them from the window of his apartment, taken into the street, and shot on the spot.

The earliest information on the music of China is the treatise of the Père Amiot, one of the Jesuit missionaries to that country, forming the sixth volume of the *Mémoires concernant l'Histoire, les Sciences, etc., des Chinois* (Paris, 1780 : 15 vols., 4to), of which a few copies were printed with a separate title, dated 1779. The facts and the illustrations given in this work have been used by every subsequent writer. The manuscript of the book was sent from China by the author to M. Bertin, Minister and Secretary of State, and was edited, annotated, and passed through the press, by the Abbé Roussier. The writer's copy is the original one which belonged to the Abbé, and is further enriched by many notes in his handwriting. But it has another special point of interest. All through the notes, the author is referred to as "le Père Amiot"; in 1764, however, the Society of Jesus had been suppressed in France. There is bound in at the end of the volume a letter from the secretary of M. Bertin, in the following terms :—

" M. Bertin, Monsieur, a remarqué que M. Amiot etoit appellé dans vos notes

sur la Musique *le P. Amiot.* Je vous
serais obligé de vouloir bien corriger cette
faute dans le reste de l'ouvrage, et faire
imprimer M. Amiot au lieu de le P.
Amiot. Les Jesuites n' existant plus."

Another letter follows, waiving the
objection, as the sheets were already
printed off ; a note is added in Roussier's
handwriting, to state that the requisite
correction was made in the index.

The learned Orientalist, Sir William
Jones, was the first to give any account of
Music in India. His paper "On the
Musical Modes of the Hindus" was
originally contributed to the *Asiatic Researches* (vol. iii., p. 55), and afterwards
included in his collected works. A translation into German was made by Baron
Dablerg, who had paid much attention to
the subject, and was able to add con-
siderably to the value of the researches
of Sir W. Jones. In this form the work
is much more readily procured. The
writer has never seen Willard's *Treatise
on the Music of Hindoostan* (Calcutta,
1834 : 8vo), which Fétis says "is super-
ficial." In later years Rajah Sir Sourindro
Mohun Tagore, Mus. Doc., a well-qualified
musician, has published several works on
the subject.

In addition to the numerous works we

have mentioned, there remain some which, while not deserving the title of histories, form valuable sources of information as being contemporary records. Italy is not rich in works of this nature, but some interesting matter is to be found in a little treatise of Pietro della Valle, *Della Musica dell' eta nostra*, included in the magnificent edition of the works of G. B. Doni, edited by Gori a century and a quarter after his decease (Florence, 1773 : 2 vols., folio).

The literature of France is richer in contemporary records. The first to be mentioned is a work of a very curious nature. A certain M. Titon du Tillet conceived the idea of erecting a monument to the glory of Louis XIV., and of all the great men of his reign. It was to be called "Le Parnasse François," and was to be executed on a large scale in bronze. Probably funds were not forthcoming for so magnificent a scheme, but a model was exhibited in the Bibliothéque Royal, at Paris. A description of the work was published in a handsome folio volume, *Le Parnasse François* (Paris, 1732), with several supplements. In addition to a description of the monument, biographies are given of the eminent persons represented in it. Among the musicians thus honoured are the Couperins, Lully, Collasse, Marais, Montéclair, the Philidors, and others of less note. The work had been preceded by a volume, identical in plan, but on a smaller scale, *Description du Parnasse François* (Paris, 1727 : 12mo).

The other French work which we have to mention is the *Essai sur la Musique Ancienne et Moderne* (Paris, 1780 : 4 vols., 4to), published anonymously, the privilege even being granted to *Notre amé le sieur* . . ., but which is well known to have been compiled by—or perhaps it would be more correct to say, under the auspices of—J. B. de la Borde, one of the farmers general, who, like so many of his order, perished by the guillotine, a few days only before the fall of Robespierre. La Borde has come into notice during the last few years on the strength of a collection of songs in four volumes, octavo, which has lately been fetching ridiculous prices at sales, on account of the engravings with which it is illustrated. The *Essai* is also tastefully printed and illustrated with excellent engravings, of which the head-pieces of the chapters are specially charming. The literary part of the work is unfortunately not so admirable, and it has been described as a " *chef d'oeuvre* of ignorance, disorder, and carelessness." La

Borde's share in the work consisted mainly in supplying the funds, and in exercising a general supervision. The materials were collected by a number of writers, a certain Bêche, one of three brothers, members of the King's Band, having a large share in the work, while the Abbé Roussier is answerable for the theoretical portion. The result is a strange jumble of ill-arranged information, much of which is of very doubtful authority. Vol. iii. contains a series of short accounts of the musicians of different countries, arranged alphabetically, those of each nation separately. The list of Italian composers is a long one, and the information it contains was not readily to be found elsewhere at that time. This is followed by lists of poets and performers, and another of theoretical writers. Chapters viii.—x. of this volume are devoted to French musicians, among whom Lully is, of course, included; and it is here that the value of the work is concentrated, for it forms the principal source of our information on Music in France during that period. The fourth volume is principally devoted to French lyric poets, with some information supplementary to that in the previous volume. With all its faults, there is a certain

pleasure in turning over the pages of so
well printed a book, on which no expense
was spared; most of the copies also are
bound in contemporary French calf,
which it is a delight to look upon.

Our knowledge of the lives of the
earlier German musicians is largely
derived from Mattheson's *Grundlage
einer Ehrenpforte* (Hamburg, 1740 : 4to),
which forms, with Walther's *Lexicon*, to
be noticed later, the principal source of
information. The work is a series of
biographies, arranged alphabetically, of
eminent German musicians. The author
is careful to distinguish the sources from
which his information is derived. When
the master was still living, he applied to
him direct for his facts, drawing up his
account from the information given. In
this way he applied to his old friend
Handel, who, however, refused or neglected to supply the desired particulars.
Mattheson's acquaintance among his
contemporaries was a wide one, and the
period was important in the history of
German music, which makes this somewhat scarce book a desirable possession.

M. E. Van der Straeten's *La Musique
aux Pays-Bas*, of which eight volumes have
already appeared (Brussels, 1867, etc.:
8vo), contains much valuable informa-

tion on the progress of the art in those countries. It is emphatically "materials for history," the result of the writer's laborious researches among public and other documents, printed with but little arrangement, apparently direct from his commonplace book. The author was for a time secretary to Fétis, and subsequently engaged in the "Archives" of Brussels.

Hardly separable from history are the biographies of musicians, which go so far to form the materials of the former. Of nearly every musician of eminence a published biography is to be found, and of the more famous there is a choice. It is obviously impossible to treat of this subject fully—to do so would require a volume larger than the present ; we will, however, mention a few of the more important, and for further imformation must refer the reader to the pages of Fétis or Grove, both of whom indicate the principal sources of information.

It is remarkable that the first serious attempt at a life of Handel should have proceeded from a Frenchman living in this country—Victor Schoelcher—(London, 1857 : 8vo). The author was an indifferent musician, and his critical judgment was not trustworthy, but the work contains much interesting information. The great Handel scholar, Dr. Chrysander, embarked on a life of the composer, but it has stood still for many years in the middle of the third volume, and will now probably be never completed. Mr. Rockstro is answerable for an admirable biography (London, 1883 : 8vo), while, on a smaller scale, that of Mrs. Julian Marshall in the "Great Musicians" series is excellent, forming one of a valuable little collection.

Of Handel's great contemporary J. S. Bach, apart from notices in musical journals (and of these the most important is that by Bach's son Emanuel and his pupil Agricola, to be found in Mitzler's *Musikalische Bibliothek* (1734)), the first attempt at a biography was that of Forkel— *Johann Sebastian Bach's Leben, Kunst, und Kunstwerke* (Leipzig, 1802 : 4to), of which an English translation has been published (London, 1820 : 8vo) ; but the authoritative biography is that by Spitta (Leipzig, 1873–80 : 2 vols., 8vo), of which an excellent translation by Miss C. Bell and Mr. Fuller-Maitland has been published by Messrs. Novello (1884–5 : 3 vols., 8vo).

The biography of Haydn was the occasion of a most remarkable instance of literary dishonesty. In the year 1814 appeared in Paris, *Lettres écrites de Vienne en Autriche sur le célèbre compositeur Jf. Haydn, suivies d'une vie de Mozart et de considérations sur Métastase,* purporting to be by Louis Alexandre César Bombet. The person really answerable for the volume was Marie Henri Beyle, who afterwards achieved some celebrity as a writer, and was without doubt a man of ability. The work was no sooner published than a well-known musical *littérateur,* Giuseppe Carpani, recognised it as a barefaced appropriation of his own work on Haydn, whose intimacy he enjoyed, entitled *Le Haydine* (Milan, 1812 : 8vo). The plagiarism was at once exposed, for it was incontestible. Most men with such a charge brought home to them would have courted obscurity by withdrawing the work. Not so M. Beyle ; he made no attempt at a reply, but in 1817 positively had the effrontery to publish a second edition—this time under a new pseudonym, that of De Stendhal. An English translation of the work appeared in 1817, by Robert Brewin, of Leicester, with notes by William Gardiner, the enthusiastic amateur and stocking weaver of the same town, who sent Haydn a present of stockings, with subjects from the composer's works woven in ! Nor did M. Beyle stop here. In 1823 he produced a *Vie de Rossini* (Paris: 8vo), again under the name of Stendhal, a large part of which was "conveyed" from letters contributed by Carpani to Italian and German newspapers. No complete life of Haydn exists. C. F. Pohl, the learned librarian of the Gesellschaft der Musick-freunde in Vienna, has treated of a portion of the composer's life with great detail in his *Mozart und Haydn in London* (Vienna, 1867 : 2 vols., 8vo), and has also published two volumes of a biography of the master (Leipzig, 1875 : 8vo); but it is scarcely probable that the work will ever be completed.

The charm of Mozart's personality has proved very attractive to biographers. Neglecting mere obituary notices, the earliest in the field was Franz Niemtschek with the *Leben des Kapellmeisters Wolfgang Gottlieb Mozart* (Prag, 1798 : 4to)— little more than a pamphlet, of which a second edition appeared in 1808 : 8vo. In 1803 J. E. F. Arnold published his *Mozart's Geist* (Erfurt : 8vo). But no adequate biography appeared until that by Nissen (Leipzig, 1828 : 8vo, with a supplement). The author, Danish *chargé d'affaires* at Vienna, who married the

Composer's widow, spent five-and-twenty years in collecting and arranging his materials, but did not live to see the work through the press. In spite of this devotion to the subject, the work is a collection of materials—of the highest value, indeed—rather than a biography. It was translated into several languages. The delightful *Life of Mozart*, by Edward Holmes (London, 1845 : 8vo ; 2nd edition, *ib.*, 1878, with the addition of excellent notes by Professor Prout), is based on it ; there is a French translation by Albert Sowinski (Paris, 1869 : 8vo), and the Abbé Goschler brought out an abridgment with the curious title, *Mozart : Vie d'un artiste chrétien* (Paris, 1857 : 12mo). Nissen's work was followed, in 1843, by the *Nouvelle Biographie de Mozart* of the enthusiastic Russian amateur, Alexander von Oulibicheff—so idolatrous an admirer of the Composer that he was quite incapable of recognising merit elsewhere. The book was published at Moscow in three octavo volumes, in the French language, and is now rarely met with, but it is obtainable in a German translation, of which several editions have appeared (Stuttgart, 1847, etc. ; 3 or 4 vols., 8vo). It may be interesting to point out that the numerous musical examples are, in the original edition, engraved on wood, thus going back to the earliest method of reproducing music. The most exhaustive, and it may be said the standard, book is Otto Jahn's *W. A. Mozart* (Leipzig, 1856–9 : 4 vols. ; 2nd edition, 2 vols., 1862). This also has been well translated by Pauline D. Townsend, and published by Messrs. Novello (London, 1882 : 3 vols., 8vo).

Mozart himself has furnished a large portion of the materials for his own life in the very charming series of letters which he left behind. Nissen's work, and that of Jahn, contain a large selection of them, but they were added to by the collection published by Ludwig Nohl (Leipzig, 1865 : 8vo), excellently translated by Lady Wallace. Nohl added several volumes to the Mozart literature.

The reader will remember the curious history of Mozart's *Requiem*, and the controversy with regard to its authenticity. The subject will be found admirably summed up in *The Story of Mozart's Requiem*, by William Pole, F.R.S. (London, 1879 : 8vo).

Of Beethoven, the earliest biographies were the *Biographische Notizen* by Wegeler and Ries (Coblentz, 1838 : 8vo), and Schindler's *Biographie* (Münster,

1840 : 8vo), of which Moscheles's *Life* (London, 1841 : 2 vols., 8vo) is little more than a translation. Works on a larger scale were issued by Marx and Ludwig Nohl, but the most important is that by A. W. Thayer, *Ludwig von Beethoven's Leben* (Berlin 1866-79 : 3 vols., 8vo). Mr. Thayer is an American who has devoted himself with great singleness of purpose to the study of the subject, and his work is of the utmost value. Unfortunately the three volumes already published only carry us down to 1816, so that eleven years of the great Composer's life remain unchronicled. The work was written in English, but issued in a German translation, with a view to inviting criticism, of which the author proposed to avail himself before publishing his definite edition in the English language. It is a little remarkable that there should be no adequate life of Beethoven in our own language—for that of Moscheles does not satisfy modern requirements. Of very great interest to the student of the master are his sketch-books, first laid open to the public by G. Nottebohm in his *Skizzenbuch von Beethoven* (Leipzig, 1863 : 8vo), and in his *Beethoveniana* (Leipzig, 1872 and 1887 : 8vo). The reader is enabled to see how gradual was the development of many of Beethoven's greatest and apparently most spontaneous works, and how rigid was the criticism which he brought to bear on his own composition. Never was genius more emphatically "the art of taking infinite pains."

The division of the works of Beethoven into three periods was first suggested by Fétis in the first edition of his *Biographie Universelle*, but the idea was caught up and elaborated by the Russian amateur Lenz, in his *Beethoven et ses trois styles* (St. Petersburg, 1852 : 2 vols., 8vo ; but more frequently met with in the French reprint, Paris, 1855). The book is an enthusiastic rhapsody, in which the author takes occasion to attack Oulibicheff for his exclusive devotion to Mozart and his inability to appreciate the later works of Beethoven, when he had shaken himself free from the style of the earlier composer. Oulibicheff replied in his *Beethoven, ses critiques et ses glossateurs* (Paris, 1857 : 8vo) ; but the controversy embittered his existence and is said to have shortened his life, for he died in the following year.

Schubert's life has been written by Kreissle von Hellborn (Vienna, 1865 : 8vo), translated into English by Mr. A. D.

Coleridge (London, 1869 : 2 vols., 8vo), and epitomised by Mr. Wilberforce (London, 1866 : 8vo), but the best information is without doubt contained in the article by Sir G. Grove in his *Dictionary*, whose articles on Mendelssohn and Schumann, in the same work, are also excellent. Both Mendelssohn and Schumann may be said to await a definitive biography, although many materials for it have, in each case, been given to the world. Among the most interesting in the case of the former composer are the two charming series of letters, *Reisebriefe aus den Jahren* 1830 *bis* 1832 (Leipzig, 1861 : 8vo), and *Briefe aus den Jahren* 1833 *bis* 1847 (*ib.*, 1863 : 8vo). Both of these have been translated into English by Lady Wallace (London, 1862, 1863 : 8vo). Mendelssohn's sunny nature shines through all his letters, and they form delightful reading, even to those not specially interested in music. The same may be said of Hensel's *Die Familie Mendelssohn* (Berlin, 1879 : 3 vols., 8vo), an interesting account of a highly cultivated family. It has been translated into English by K. Klingemann (London, 1881 : 2 vols., 8vo). Mendelssohn was so prominent a figure in the musical world up to the time of his premature decease, and his character was so attractive, that all the memoirs of that period are full of references to him. Some of the most interesting are contained in Madame Moscheles' *Aus Moscheles Leben* (Leipzig, 1872-3: 2 vols., 8vo), translated into English by A. D. Coleridge (London, 1873: 2 vols., 8vo).

Of Schumann, the fullest life is that by Wasielewski—*Robert Schumann, seine Biographie* (Dresden, 1858: 8vo; with subsequent editions). This has been translated by A. Alger (London, 1878: 8vo). Spohr's *Autobiography* (Cassel, 1860-61: 2 vols., 8vo; English translation, London [but printed in Germany], 1865: 8vo) will be found most entertaining reading; it is full of real interest, but tinctured with the most delightful self-complacency. Finally, Chopin must be mentioned. The earliest work on his life was that of Liszt—*Frédéric Chopin*—written in French, but first published in book form at Leipzig (Breitkopf, 1882: 8vo), although it was rather a critical study than a biography, the first systematic attempt at which was M. Karasowski's *Frederick Chopin; seine Leben, seine Werke und seine Briefe* (Dresden, 1887: 8vo). Of both these works there are English translations. In 1888 Mr. F.

Niecks brought out his *Frederick Chopin as a man and musician* (London : 2 vols., 8vo), an exhaustive work, probably containing all we are likely to know of the great musician. It is right to add that the author does not satisfy those who are more anxious to have depicted a Chopin, and a George Sand, who conform to their own ideals rather than to the testimony of contemporary evidence.

M. Pougin, the well-known editor of the continuation of the *Biographie* of Fétis has been a most industrious biographer of musicians, mainly French. This author's life of Verdi, originally contributed to the *Ménestrel* in 1878 was soon afterwards translated into Italian (by Folchetto), and also into Spanish and German. In 1886 M. Pougin brought out a new edition, which was translated into English by the compiler of this volume, and it has also been translated into German.

An excellent series of *Masters of English, French, German, and Italian Music* (London, 1893-5 : 4 vols., 8vo) has been published. The respective volumes are by Messrs. C. Willeby, A. Hervey, J. A. Fuller-Maitland and R. A. Streatfield. These treat of contemporary musicians. Mr. W. H. Hadow has published two series of really admirable *Studies in Modern Music.* The author's critical powers place him among the foremost musical writers of the day. And we must here mention Mr. Hubert Parry's *Art of Music* (London, 1894 : 8vo), which is virtually a history of the development of Musical Form. It is a work of the first importance, showing a masterly grasp of the subject, and should be in the hands of every student.

The history of Musical Notation is well traced by E. David and M. Lussy, in their *Histoire de la Notation Musicale* (Paris, 1882 : folio).

CHAPTER VII.

DICTIONARIES OF MUSIC.

E now come to the consideration of a large and a useful class of musical literature—the Dictionaries of Music, which range themselves under three groups—technical dictionaries, biographical dictionaries, and those which endeavour to combine both subjects.

It has already been pointed out that Music was the earliest of the arts to possess a special dictionary—the *Diffinitorium Musicæ* of Tinctoris, published, it is believed, as early as 1474, the interest of which now is purely antiquarian. But it is equally remarkable that, although such terms as fell within the scope of his work are explained in the well-known *Glossarium* of Ducange, no second attempt of the kind should have been made till the year 1701, when Thomas Balthazar Janowka, an organist at Prague, published his *Clavis ad Thesaurum magnæ artis*

Musicæ (Prague, 1701 : 8vo). The book
is of very great rarity, and the writer has
never seen it; but as it contains three
hundred and twenty-four pages, the subject must have been treated with some
detail. A copy is in the Fétis library at
Brussels.

This publication was followed up almost
immediately in France by the *Dictionnaire
de Musique, contenant une Explication
des termes grecs, latins, italiens et françois,
les plus usitez dans la Musique,* by Sebastien
de Brossard (Paris, 1703 : folio). The
work is disposed in two alphabets, the
first devoted to Italian terms, the second
to French, together with such Greek and
Latin words as are current in the art.
The work is of great excellence for the
time when it appeared, and it must be
remembered that it was entirely original,
and that the author had no previous work
of a like nature to guide him in the
selection of terms and subjects to be
handled—a selection made with considerable completeness. The alphabetical
part is succeeded by a treatise on the
manner of pronouncing Italian words,
and then follows one of the earliest attempts to form a bibliography of books
on Music, which is of the greatest interest.
The folio edition is far from common,

but a second edition appeared in Paris in 1705 (8vo), and a third at Amsterdam (probably pirated) by Estienne Roger, without date, which is frequently to be met with, and is worth acquiring.

If England was well to the front in the production of histories of Music, it was not far behind with dictionaries of the subject. In 1724 appeared *A Short Explication of such Foreign Words as are made Use of in Musick Books*. As the preface states, it was "not intended for the Use of Masters, but only for such Gentlemen and Ladies who, being Lovers of Musick, nevertheless may possibly be ignorant of the true Signification of many of the said Terms." It is a pretty little duodecimo volume of ninety-six pages, and as the type is rather large for the size of the page, there is no room for very long explanations ; but they are sensible and accurate, and there is added an interesting appendix, giving lists of music printed for various instruments. The writer is quite at a loss to assign the authorship of this interesting little work.

But this was soon followed by a work of larger proportions and more important aims—the *Musical Dictionary ; being a collection of Terms and Characters as well ancient as modern, by James Grassineau,*

Gent. (London, 1740 : 8vo). The author was born in London, of French parents, and, after a period of less congenial occupation, became secretary to Dr. Pepusch, and by his advice he undertook the translation of Brossard's Dictionary. It was on this translation that Grassineau's work was based, but with many modifications and additions which gave it a value of its own. The compiler expresses his obligations to Dr. Pepusch, and it is generally supposed that much of the additional matter was supplied by him.

The Dictionary of Music which has been most talked about, and most often reprinted, is, without doubt, that of Jean Jacques Rousseau, first published at Geneva in 1767 (4to). In the preface to this work the author explains the circumstances which induced him to undertake it. Rousseau's knowledge of the science of Music was neither deep nor accurate, and it was on account of his friendly relations with Diderot and D'Alembert that he was selected to undertake the musical part of the famous *Encyclopédie*, to the great chagrin of Rameau, whose qualifications were so much more commanding. The time allowed for the completion of these articles was insufficient to allow their author to engage in the preliminary studies which his indifferent acquaintance with the subject rendered necessary. Rousseau himself recognised their deficiences, and, having taken up his residence in Switzerland, decided on devoting his time to re-casting his materials and to the production of a work of more solid value.

It will be admitted that Rousseau's mind was not of the cast to qualify him for such a task. The remarkable popularity of the *Dictionnaire* has depended rather on its literary merits, which make it interesting reading. His love and taste for Music were undoubted, and give to his critical articles a certain value. It is well known that for ·a long period of his life Rousseau supported himself as a music copyist ; his practical acquaintance with the art makes the article *Copiste* one of the best, which may still be studied with advantage. The Dictionary was reprinted many times, both separately and as forming part of his complete works ; it was also translated into most of the European languages, the English version being by William Waring.

Rousseau had numerous successors in France, the work on the largest scale being the *Dictionnaire de Musique*, forming two out of the two hundred and one volumes

quarto of the *Encyclopédie Méthodique.*
The first volume, published in 1791, was
edited by Framéry and Ginguené, both of
whom were better known as *littérateurs*
than as musicians. They were assisted in
the theoretical part of the work by the
Abbé Feytou. It is avowedly based on
the Dictionary of Rousseau, with many of
whose views, however, the compilers were
at variance, nor did they agree among
themselves, so that many of the articles
are contradictory. Ginguené was answerable for the historical notices, in compiling
which he was greatly indebted to Burney's
History. The publication of the work
was interrupted by the troubles of the
Revolution, and it was not till 1818 that
the second volume appeared, with the
name of De Momigny added to those of
the previous editors; but at that date
both Framéry and Ginguené were dead,
so that the whole responsibility of the
volume devolved on Momigny, who had
a theory of his own, entirely opposed to
the views expressed in the earlier volume,
which he advances in season and out of
season. The result is that the huge work
of eleven hundred and twenty closely
printed pages of double columns, with a
hundred and fourteen pages of examples, is
a very blind guide. It must be mentioned

as a merit that the principal articles are signed.

No good purpose would be served by enumerating all the dictionaries which have been compiled from time to time, both in France and England, for most of which no critical value can be claimed. We may mention those of Castil-Blaze and of the brothers Escudier as having had a wide circulation in France, while in our own country the *Dictionary* of Busby was frequently reprinted, answering the demands of the ordinary inquirer, till it was superseded by more modern works, among the best of which is that of Dr. H. Hiles.   But a truly admirable *Dictionary of Musical Terms* was some years back published by Messrs. Novello, edited by Sir John Stainer and Mr. W. A. Barrett, assisted by a few specialists, which is far in advance of any such work previously brought out.   It is indispensable to every musician, as it is no mere compilation, but the result of much original research, conveyed in clear and succinct language, and well abreast of the scientific discoveries of the day.   Our only complaint (and that does not touch the merits of the book) is that it is issued without a date.

The Land of Song possessed no dictionary of Music till the publication of the Abbate Pietro Gianelli's *Dizionario* in 1801 (Venice : 3 vols., 8vo). In this first edition of the work the author included notices of some of the principal musicians, but they are very imperfect. For instance, all he finds to say about Handel is that an example in his *Suite de pièces* proves that the fourth is not a dissonant interval— that he was a celebrated composer, and that we have of his, twelve celebrated chamber duets ! The existence of his oratorios seems quite unsuspected ! In the second edition (Venice, 1820), the work was extended to seven very thin volumes, and the author had the good sense to leave out his inadequate biographical notices.

Italy produced one excellent dictionary of Music, although the author was a Hungarian. This is the *Dizionario e Bibliografia della Musica* of Dr. Pietro Lichtenthal (Milan, 1826). With the bibliography, of which we shall have to speak later, the work occupies four volumes octavo, two of which are devoted to the dictionary. The author, who was a physician, was a very earnest and careful student of Music, and his work may be consulted with advantage. A French translation of it was made by D. Mondo (Paris, 1839 : 2 vols., 8vo).

In Germany the plan of combining the

technical and the biographical dictionaries seems to have been preferred. The earliest dictionary not comprising biography is that of G. F. Wolf (Halle, 1787 : 8vo), with subsequent editions in 1792 and 1806. This was followed, in 1802, by the *Musikalisches Lexikon* of H. C. Koch (Frankfurt-on-Main, 1802 : 8vo), a scientific and well-informed writer. It is a work on a large scale, comprising over eighteen hundred columns, adapted to the needs of advanced students. Koch himself published an abridgment of his work, under the title of *Kurzgefasstes Handwörterbuch der Musik* (Leipzig, 1807 : 8vo), also a useful and popular work, which maintained its position for a long time, an edition purporting to be Koch's dictionary having been issued by Arrey von Dommer so late as 1865, in which, however, but little of the original remains. In a country where music is so much studied as in Germany, there has been, of course, a constant supply of dictionaries adapted to the wants of young students, which need not be spoken of here.

There exist a few technical dictionaries devoted to special departments of musical knowledge. Among these must be mentioned the *Wörterbuch der griechischen Musik* of F. von Drieberg (Berlin, 1835 :

4to), the scope of which is sufficiently indicated by its title, and a truly remark-work, the *Dictionnaire de Plain-Chant et de Musique d'Eglise*, by Joseph d'Ortigue (Paris, 1853 : large 8vo). This forms the twenty-seventh volume of the well-known *Encyclopédie Théologique*, published by the Abbé Migne, who has been so instrumental in bringing the works of the Fathers within the means of those who are not in a position to acquire Benedictine editions. The various subjects are treated exhaustively, and the work is indispensable to those who are interested in such matters. It is, of course, designed for the use of members of the Roman Church. Equally valuable, from a different point of view, is the *Dictionary of Hymnology* (London, 1892 : large 8vo), a colossal undertaking, for which our thanks are due both to the editor, the Rev. J. Julian, and his able assistants, as well as to the publisher, Mr. Murray, for bringing such an enterprise to so successful an issue.

We now come to dictionaries devoted exclusively to the biography of musicians. The earliest of these is the *Historisch-Biographisches Lexicon*, of Ernst Ludwig Gerber (Leipzig, 1790 and 1792 : 2 vols., 8vo), which is really the parent of all subsequent undertakings of a like nature. The work had its origin in a desire to extend and complete the labours of Walther, who had compiled a dictionary both technical and biographical, of which we shall have to speak later. Fifteen years were occupied in collecting materials, in which the author was assisted by J. A. Hiller, Forkel, and Ebeling. The manuscript was shown to Breitkopf by Hiller, who at once saw the value of the work, and engaged Gerber to complete and produce it. The result was the dictionary of 1790 and 1792, which, however, was not entirely satisfactory, although it had a large circulation. Many errors, almost inseparable from a work of this kind, had crept in—errors in dates, omissions, double articles, really referring to the same person, and actual mistakes. But the compiler was both modest and industrious, and he did not cease to collect material, which he subsequently embodied in his *Neues historisch-biographi- sches Lexikon* (Leipzig, 1812-14: 4 vols., 8vo). It must be understood that this second work does not supersede the first, but consists of additions and corrections. The earlier book is constantly referred to, and must be at hand to enable the student to make full use of the second. It contains a very valuable and useful table of published portraits of musicians, giving both painter and engraver, and this is supplemented in the more recent dictionary.

The success of this book suggested to the well-known French musician, Choron, the issue of a similar work, a prospectus of which he issued. This came to the notice of Fayolle, who had been making collections with the same object. He acquainted Choron with the fact, and they very wisely arranged to combine their labours. In the meantime Choron fell ill, so that, with the exception of the historical summary prefixed to the dictionary, and one or two articles, Fayolle became answerable for the whole, which appeared at Paris in 1810 and 1811: 2 vols., 8vo. Part of the edition was issued with a title, dated 1817. A large portion of the work is simply a translation of Gerber, and it cannot be looked on as of much authority.

The writer has never been able to ascertain who were the compilers of our English *Dictionary of Musicians* (London, 1824 : 2 vols., 8vo ; 2nd edition, 1827), which frankly confesses its obligations to Gerber, Choron and Fayolle, and other works. Such value as the work possesses is dependent mainly on the information given about native musicians. The *Dizionario storico-critico* of the Abbate Giuseppe Bertini (Palermo, 1814 and 1815 : 4 vols., small 4to) owes its origin to the same sources, but has some original matter on Italian musicians.

But all these works are virtually superseded by one which is absolutely indispensable to every musical student—the *Biographie universelle des Musiciens* of F. J. Fétis. The first edition of this great work appeared in Brussels in 1835-44 : 8 vols., 8vo. This issue is, of course, set aside by the more recent edition, Paris, 1860-65, but it still has a value, on account of the excellent *Résumé Philosophique* before alluded to. This edition, it must be acknowledged, is full of blunders, especially in the notices of English musicians, which are very inadequate, and mainly taken from the *Biographical Dictionary of* 1824. In 1860 Fétis began the issue of a second edition, which he completed in 1865 in eight volumes. Nothing comparable to this remarkable work has appeared either before or since. The erudition and research which it displays are wonderful. Nevertheless, Fétis is very far from being a perfectly satisfactory guide. His self-confidence was absolute ; any one who differed

from his views was *wrong*. From his judgment there was no appeal ! This master-
fulness is a little apt to impose on the reader
till experience teaches him that the author's
statements are frequently coloured by his
own opinions, and that his dates require
further investigation. Nor was he, as we
have before remarked, willing to acknowledge assistance rendered by others—in
fact, he was not above using such sources
of information as a means of attack on the
giver. But, with all these faults, there is
no other book to take its place ; and those
who, like the writer, have had occasion to
consult it almost daily for many years past,
must be lost in admiration at the depth
and extent of knowledge which it displays.

With the lapse of years a supplement
was, of course, called for. This has been
admirably supplied by M. Arthur Pougin
in 1878, 1880 : 2 vols., 8vo. M. Pougin
called to his assistance a number of capable writers, and adopted the excellent
plan of adding their signatures to the
articles. The possessor of the original
work (and it is one of the first which the
student should acquire) will not fail to
add these two volumes.

The *Biographical Dictionary of Musicians* by Mr. J. D. Brown (Paisley, 1886 :
8vo), formerly of the Mitchell Library,

Glasgow, but now of the Clerkenwell Library, one of our most capable librarians, was scarcely received with the attention it deserved. It is a most painstaking work. The biographical notices are succinct, and to each is appended a really excellent bibliography of the works of the composer. It is especially good in notices of recent English musicians, and much information which will be looked for in vain in other works will be found here. Mr. David Baptie's *Handbook of Musical Biography* (London, [1883]: 8vo) confines itself to the barest facts, but it is a useful little work, and, the writer has reason to think, very accurate in dates. Both Mr. Baptie and Mr. W. H. Cummings have also issued alphabetical lists, confining the information to the nature of the composer's work and the dates of his birth and death, which is carrying compression almost too far.

Without professing to have exhausted the purely biographical dictionaries, we have mentioned the most important and the most useful. There is another class which may be also consulted with advantage : dictionaries devoted to the musicians of a particular town or country. Of these there are several. The earliest was the *Baierisches Musik Lexikon* of

F. J. Lipowsky (Munich, 1811 : 8vo).
In 1846 and 1847 appeared the *Schlesisches
Tonkünstler-Lexikon* of Kossmaly and
Carlo, devoted to the musicians of Silesia.
(Breslau : 8vo). The information is said
to be trustworthy, but the arrangement is
most inconvenient. It was issued in four
parts, each containing an entire alphabet,
so that four references are sometimes
necessary to ascertain whether a name
is included. In addition to the biographies of musicians, it gives accounts of
the various musical societies belonging
to the Province. In 1857 Albert Sowinski, a capable and esteemed Polish
musician, resident in Paris, published
*Les Musiciens Polonais et Slaves, anciens
et modernes, Dictionnaire Biographique*
(Paris : 8vo), a work of very great research,
indispensable to those who wish to investigate the musical history of this richly
endowed nation. The musicians of Berlin
found an admirable biographer in Carl
von Ledebur, whose *Tonkünstler-Lexikon
Berlins* appeared in that city in 1861, in a
large octavo volume of over seven hundred
pages. We are particular in giving these
details, as at the time Fétis wrote his
notice of Ledebur the work was incomplete, and Fétis appears to have supposed
that it was destined to remain so. It

contains living as well as deceased musicians, and much of it is based on original investigations, so that its value is considerable.   Even such small cities as Lübeck, in North Germany, and Salzburg, in Austria, have their special dictionaries by Stiehl (Lübeck, 1821 : 8vo) and Pillwein (Salzburg, 1821 : 8vo).

For the musicians of Spain we have the *Diccionario* of Baltasar Saldoni, the contents of which are admirable, but arranged with extraordinary perversity.   The first attempt at this work was produced in 1860 (Madrid : 1 vol., 8vo), under the title of *Efémerides de Músicos Españoles*, and, as expressed by the title, it took the unfortunate shape of a calendar, the notice of each musician being under the date of his birth, or, more frequently, of his death. This is of necessity followed by an index, with a reference to the date under which the name is treated.   When the author knows neither the date of the birth nor of the death, his system, of course, breaks down, and he is compelled to provide for such cases in a separate alphabet, which extends to almost as many pages as the *Efémerides*, although printed in much smaller type.   Why he cannot have combined the two in one general alphabet passes comprehension ; but the principle

of a calendar seems to have had a fascina-
tion for him, for in 1868 he embarked on
a greatly enlarged work, still following the
same system. This first volume of the
new attempt contains the months of
January and February only, with an
alphabetical index to each month *separately*, and a few names, beginning with the
letter *A*, of those whose births or deaths
were unknown to him. Probably the
work languished from lack of patronage,
as no further instalment appeared till
1880, when the second and third volumes
appeared, the second with supplementary
names in January and February, each
with a distinct index, but bringing the
general calendar down to June, while
the third finished the year and contained,
in addition to the index to each month,
a general index to the whole work. In
1881 the fourth and concluding volume
appeared, almost entirely devoted to an
alphabetical dictionary of names to whose
birth or death no date can be assigned. It
should be mentioned that each volume concludes with a few pages of " Variedades,"
which seem to consist of cuttings from
newspapers on such musical subjects as
interested the author. In the two sections
of the work he claims to have noticed
three thousand eight hundred and seventy-

one musicians, which is not a bad muster
for one nation.   It will be conceded that
the book is most harassing to consult,
but the information, when found, is generally trustworthy.

The dictionary of Portuguese musicians,
by Joaquim de Vasconcellos, a well-
qualified writer (*Os Musicos Portuguezes*,
Porto, 1870 : 2 vols., 8vo), is fortunately
free from any such vagaries of arrangement.   It is to be regretted that as yet
no one has been patriotic enough to
attempt a dictionary of English musicians.

We are now brought to the third class
of dictionaries of music—those which
attempt to combine the technical with
the biographical, a plan which too often
results in sacrificing much of the utility
of each.   The practice has met with
special favour in Germany.

The first attempt of this sort was the
*Musikalisches Lexicon, oder Musikalische
Bibliothec* of Johann Gottfried Walther,
a musician of great attainments and a
relation of J. S. Bach.   In 1728 he
published, or printed, a specimen of his
musical dictionary—one copy of which
only is known, that in the Fétis library—
covering the letter *A.*   Four years later
he brought out his complete work (Leipzig,

1738 : 8vo) of six hundred and sixty-eight pages, with plates of music. The work has a distinct value of its own, for with the *Ehrenpforte* of Mattheson it forms the principal source of our information about the German musicians of that period. It contains the names of musicians then living, and it is curious that, while several of the Bach family are noticed, the name of Handel does not occur. All successive labourers in the field of musical biography and bibliography are under great obligations to Walther, while the definitions and explanations of musical terms are well executed.

The writer is unable to assign the authorship of a work on a smaller scale, the *Kurzgefasstes Musicaliches Lexicon*, the first edition of which appeared in 1737, 2nd edition 1749, both at Chemnitz (sm. 8vo). It seems to be the result of independent work, and not an abridgment of Walther.

The next work of sufficient importance to be noticed is the *Encyclopädie der gesammten musikalischen Wissenschaften, oder Universal Lexicon der Tonkunst*, of which Dr. Schilling was editor, assisted by several capable musicians, among whom were Grosheim, Marx, L. Rellstab, Seyfried, and Gottfried Weber. The first volume appeared in 1835 (Stuttgart : 8vo), and the sixth, completing the original work, in 1838; but, as usual in such undertakings, a supplementary volume—and this with an " Anhang "—was called for in 1842. This work enjoyed great popularity, especially in Germany, and is still valuable, although now superseded by the *Musikalisches Conversations-Lexikon* projected by Hermann Mendel, with a well-chosen band of assistants, among who are Ferdinand David, Dorn, Naumann, Oscar Paul, Reissmann, and Tiersch. The original editor did not live to see the work completed, and the volumes after 1876 were edited by Dr. Reissman. A supplementary volume became necessary in 1883, and the whole work forms twelve large octavo volumes (Berlin, 1870–83). It is probably the best existing dictionary for general purposes, although the biographical articles are not so full as those in Fétis. A revised edition is now appearing.

As no such work existed in the English language, a great opportunity was offered to Sir George Grove in the compilation of his *Dictionary of Music and Musicians* (London, 1879–89: 4 vols., 8vo; with an index to the whole work issued separately in 1890). It cannot be said that the opportunity was fully grasped, for the work is almost as remarkable for its deficiencies as for its many and undoubted merits. It seems to have been part of the editor's plan to be entirely independent of all previous works of a like nature, to the extent even of making no comparison to ascertain whether names of importance were omitted. A long list might be drawn up of names which the searcher has a right to expect to find, but which are entirely omitted—to give one instance, that of a musician so prominent in the musical history of this country as Bononcini, an omission which had to be rectified by a note when the article on Handel came to be written. Perhaps it is unfair to complain that the scheme of the work appears to have been enlarged as it progressed, but surely a little foresight might have avoided the ridiculous circumstance that the title of the first volume announces the work as in two volumes, that of the second in three, and that of the third in four, the fourth volume being largely composed of a supplement, supplying the necessary corrections and additions to the original work. Some of the articles are altogether out of proportion to a work of this nature, and in this the editor is one of the chief offenders. The notices of Beethoven, Mendelssohn, Schubert, and Schumann, together occupy more than two hundred pages. They are undoubtedly valuable in themselves, and Sir George Grove has laboured so earnestly in the interests of Schubert's reputation that it seems perhaps ungracious to object to his exhaustive treatment of the subject, which we must consider too detailed for the position it occupies. The editor was, of course, assisted by a numerous and well-chosen staff of contributors, and the subjects have usually been wisely apportioned. The one glaring exception is that of the article on Hummel. The author of it is entitled to his own critical views, but he would have done well to consult the first music-seller's catalogue he came across before exposing his ignorance, real or affected, of what Hummel has really written.

With all these faults, the work is so truly admirable that we cannot help regretting the more keenly that a little more alertness of supervision was not exercised, for it is what is wanting that is to be regretted, and not the quality of the information given, which is almost invariably excellent—much of it also not to be found elsewhere. Among the most useful items are the lists given of the contents of the various collections of musical works—such, for example, as Boyce's *Cathedral Music,* Bodenschatz's *Florilegium Portense,* and other similar works. Many of the articles on musical instruments are in the safe and capable hands of Mr. A. J. Hipkins, who is the highest authority on the pianoforte and its progenitors. The learned articles of Mr. W. S. Rockstro on the various forms of music used in the Roman Catholic service, and on other matters, especially a very remarkable article on Schools of Music, although possibly too extended, contain information of the greatest value, nowhere previously given. The index, drawn up with infinite care and labour by Mrs. E. R. Wodehouse, forms a most useful, and indeed indispensable, addition to the work.

CHAPTER VIII.

THE LITERATURE OF SACRED MUSIC.

E have already commented on the constant stream of works on the practice of Plain-Song which flowed from the Italian press. As it forms a necessary part of the education of every ecclesiastic, no doubt each seminary has had its favourite handbook— probably the work of the professor entrusted with that part of the student's education. No good purpose would be served by giving their titles here. But there is one work which should be mentioned, as it is the only available source of original information on the subject of the Ambrosian Rite, which, as is well known, is still adhered to in Milan. This work, drawn up at the request of St. Carlo Borromeo, but not published till after the death of the author, Padre Camillo Perego, is entitled *La Regola del Canto Fermo Ambrosiano* (Milan, 1622 : 4to). It must be studied by any one who wishes to understand the distinctions between the Roman and the Ambrosian Chant.

The most important work on the subject of Plain-Chant published in France was *La Science et la Pratique du Plain Chant . . . par un Religieux Benedictin de la Congregation de S. Maur* (Paris, 1673: 4to). The "Religieux" was Dom Jumilhac. The original edition of this work is of very great rarity, but a second edition was issued in 1847 (Paris: 4to)—a hundred and seventy-four years after the first publication—under the able editorship of MM. Théodore Nisard (the Abbé Normand) and A. le Clercq, who have added many valuable notes. The *Traité historique et pratique sur le chant ecclesiastique . . . suivant l'usage du diocèse de Paris* (Paris, 1741: 8vo), by the Abbé Lebeuf, is interesting, on account of its historical portion, tracing the variations in Plain-Song which had established themselves in different parts of France, although it must be followed with some caution. The practical part was by the Abbé Chastelain. Another work of importance is the *Traité théorique et pratique du Plain-Chant, appelé gregorien* of the Abbé Poisson (Paris, 1750: 8vo).

The issue of the second edition of Dom Jumilhac marks a period of extraordinary revival of interest in the subject which manifested itself in France, as evidenced by the labours of such men as Fétis, La Fage, Félix Clement, the Abbé Normand, Père Lambillotte, and Danjou ; the latter started a paper—*Le Revue de la Musique religieuse* (Paris, 1845–54 : 8vo ; but it was suspended by the Revolution of 1848 for a long interval). La Fage drew up a *Cours complet de Plain-Chant* (Paris, 1855–6 : 2 vols., 8vo), and all the above, with other workers, entered with much energy into the controversy which the attempt to restore the true ancient tradition aroused, resulting in a plentiful crop of pamphlets, which it is impossible to detail here. In Germany, at about the same time, a similar movement, more quietly carried on, was in progress. It centred in the city of Regensburg, under the fostering care of Carolus Proske, to whom we are indebted for the magnificent collection of Church music known as *Musica Divina.*

The training of priests of the Roman faith was for so long a time penal in this country that there is a remarkable absence of handbooks of Plain-Song until comparatively recent times. The only book on the subject known to the writer is *An Essay on the Church Plain-Chant*

(London, 1782 : 8vo), published anonymously, "with approbation"; but with
the advance of the Oxford movement in
the Church of England "Gregorians" were
suddenly received with remarkable favour
by the more ecstatic members of the
school, and several works appeared, explaining their principles. Among the
best and earliest of these was the *Concise
Explanation of the Church Modes*, by
Charles Child Spencer (London, 1846 :
4to).

The history of religious music has a
considerable literature. To speak first
of the music of the Roman Church, we
have the *De Cantu et Musica sacra* of the
excellent Prince Abbot Martin Gerbert
(St. Blaise, 1774 : 2 vols. 4to), a work
of great erudition, which forms the basis
of most subsequent attempts. It is a
mine of wealth, and although in some
particulars corrected by the scholarship
of modern times, an honour to the man
and the age which produced it. To this
work should be added the same writer's
Vetus Liturgia Alemannica (St. Blaise,
1776 : 2 vols., 4to, paged continuously),
although more particularly devoted to
ritual.

The *Histoire Générale de la Musique
religieuse* of M. Félix Clément is a series

of articles on various periods of musical history, and on topics connected with Church music, rather than a true history. A large portion of the work is taken up with an account of liturgical dramas in churches, and the author's devotion to Plain-Song seems to blind him to the merits of Palestrina and his school. The *Geschichte der Kirchenmusik* of Raymond Schlecht (Regensburg, 1871: 8vo) answers much more accurately to its title, and is illustrated with a large number of musical examples.

The important part which the Monastery of St. Gall played in early times, in the diffusion of Plain-Song, is well known. An excellent monograph on the subject has been written by P. Anselm Schubiger, with the title of *Die Sängerschule St. Gallens vom achten bis zwölftes-Jahrhundert* (Einsieldeln and New York, 1858: 4to), illustrated with several facsimiles of portions of manuscripts preserved in that rich library, as well as other examples. And we may also here mention the admirable photographic facsimiles of ancient musical manuscripts which are being issued by the Benedictines of Solesmes, principally on account of the excellent elucidatory matter which accompanies them.

Much interest, of course, gathers round the famous choir of the Vatican, for so many years the centre of all that was greatest in Church music. There are several works devoted to it, the earliest, and perhaps the most important, of which is the *Osservazioni per ben regolare il coro de i cantori della Capella Pontifica* by Andrea Adami da Bolsena, who filled the office of "maestro" of the chapel (Rome, 1711 : 4to). The work begins with a short history of the choir, and then proceeds to give particular instructions as to the ritual to be observed at all functions, ordinary or extraordinary, as far as they concern the duties of the choir. This is followed by a list of all those who have been members of the choir, and, in the case of the more celebrated, a short biography is given, and occasionally a portrait. This is a most valuable work, and in many instances forms the only source of information. Further details as to this interesting body are to be found in F. X. Haberl's *Die Romische Schola Cantorum* (Leipzig, 1888 : 8vo), a reprint from the *Vierteljahrschrift für Musikwissenschaft.* Here are to be found the rules governing the members of the chapel, and their emoluments. Much further information is given in the

Memorie storicho-critiche della vita e delle opere di Giovanni Pierlingi da Palestrina of the Abbate G. Baini (Rome, 1828 : 2 vols., 4to)—a model of what such a work should be, the title of which gives no notion of the wealth of information supplied. Baini was himself "maestro" of the chapel. The work was translated into German by Kandler, with notes by Kiesewetter (Leipzig, 1834 : 8vo).

Venice probably formed the other most important centre of Church music in Italy. On this school much important information is to be found in Winterfeld's *Johannes Gabrieli und sein Zeitalter* (Berlin, 1834 : 2 vols., 4to ; with a volume of examples, folio), and also in the careful and excellent *Storia della Musica sacra nella già Capella Ducale di San Marco in Venezia del* 1318 *al* 1797 of Francesco Caffi (Venice, 1854 : 2 vols., 8vo).

Coming to the music of the Lutheran Church in Germany, it must be obvious how largely it is indebted to the Reformer's love for the art, which shows itself so frequently in his works and in his table-talk. The reader may be glad to find the extent of his services to Music investigated in Rambach's *Ueber D. Martin Luther's Verdienst um den Kirchengesang* (Hamburg, 1813 : 8vo) ; while F. A.

Beck's *Dr. Martin Luther's Gedanken über die Musik* (Berlin, 1825 : 8vo) collects his remarks on the subject in a convenient form.

The literature of the music of the Lutheran Church virtually resolves itself into the history of the chorales, which are so strongly bound up with the religious life of the people. It has become voluminous. One of the most important works on the subject is Carl von Winterfeld's *Der evangelische Kirchengesang* (Leipzig, 1843–47 : 3 vols, 4to), in which the subject is treated with great detail, and the authorship of most of the works of this nature is carefully traced. The work is amply illustrated with examples, and is, without doubt, *the* book on the subject in its musical aspects. The *Geschichte der Kirchenlieds* of E. E. Koch, the last (3rd ?) edition of which is Stuttgart, 1866 and 1867, four volumes octavo, is more largely occupied with the consideration of the words of the chorales, although much information will also be found on the authorship of the music. Hoffmann von Fallersleben has also written a book on the subject of the Metrical German Church music earlier than Luther, with the title, *Geschichte des Deutsches Kirchenliedes bis auf Luther's Zeit*, the third edition of which (octavo) came out in Hannover, in 1861 ; while Winterfield produced a further work—*Zur Geschichte heiliger Tonkunst* (Leipzig, 1850-52 : 2 vols., 8vo)—a somewhat miscellaneous collection, which includes, among other matters, a chapter on Psalmody in England.

A truly excellent little work on the history of Church music in our own country is found in the *English Church Composers,* by W. A. Barrett, one of the " Great Musicians " series (London, 1882 : 8vo), mainly devoted to cathedral music from the Reformation to our own times. Its utility would be greatly enhanced by an index.

Two important works on Church music in England must be referred to. The first is *The Music of the Church considered in its Various Branches, Congregational and Choral,* by the Rev. John Antes La Trobe, son of the compiler of the well-known collection of sacred music (London, 1831 : 8vo)—a work far in advance of its time, an earnest plea by a lover of Music and a good practical musician, for a greater recognition of the claims of Music in God's service—which may still be read with satisfaction. The other is *The Choral Service of the United Church of England and Ireland,* by the

Rev. John Jebb, afterwards D.D., and Canon of Hereford, also an esteemed musician (London, 1843 : 8vo). It is a practical guide to the due performance of the cathedral service, which has borne good fruit in the increased reverence which has become universal in these buildings.

Mr. J. S. Curwen's *Studies of Worship-Music* must also be mentioned. It is mainly a plea for congregational singing, and contains much sound sense and many useful hints. The work is partly occupied with a description of visits to the places of worship of various denominations, which is not without interest.

Church music in Scotland should perhaps be mentioned, on account of the remarkably acrimonious controversy which broke out on the attempt to introduce the organ into public worship in that country. The discussion was supported by Drs. Candlish, Porteous, and others. A novel, even, with the title of *Cold Souls* (Edinburgh, 1876 : 8vo), was written in denunciation of the practice—a work of incredible narrow-mindedness and bigotry. The Church of England, in the days succeeding Puritan ascendency, was also agitated by the same discussion. The practice was vindicated, among others,

by the Rev. J. Newte, in a sermon
preached at Tiverton, in Devon, on the
occasion of the erection of an organ in
that parish church (London, 1696: 4to),
and further in the treatise of Henry Dod-
well, *Concerning the Lawfulness of Musick
in Holy Offices. To which is prefixed a
preface in vindication of Mr. Newte's
Sermon* (London, 1700: 8vo), a book so
learned and pedantic that it is absolutely
unreadable.

The theory of the Rev. Arthur Bedford,
in his *Temple Musick*, that the English
cathedral service is a direct derivation
from the music of the Hebrew Temple,
has been already mentioned. Very few
people have any acquaintance with the
music at present used in the synagogues,
which claims to be traditional. Those
who wish to investigate this interesting
and difficult subject will find full information in *Baal T'Fillah oder Der practische
Vorbeter* of Abraham Baer (Frankfurt
[1883]: folio). This is the second edition
of the work.

The history of the Oratorio has scarcely
received the attention it deserves. We
know of only two works specially devoted
to the subject. The first, by C. H. Bitter,
modestly claims to be only *Beiträge zur
Geschichte des Oratoriums* (Berlin, 1872:

8vo); and, indeed, it is totally deficient in arrangement, beginning with Mendelssohn, and treating subsequently of the works of Handel. It is more especially devoted to German effort in this direction. A more comprehensive and orderly work is the *Geschichte des Oratoriums* of Otto Wangemann (Demmin, 1882 : [second edition], 8vo). The work is copiously illustrated with musical examples, and contains much bibliographical information of great interest.

CHAPTER IX.

The Literature of the Opera.

ON the threshold of the consideration of the literature of the Opera, a word or two may perhaps be said as to the objection often urged against the very existence of the Opera—that to carry on the action of a drama by means of music is opposed to nature, and therefore ridiculous. One of the best known examples of the advocacy of this view is found in the series of papers by Addison in the earlier numbers of the *Spectator.* The charm and playful delicacy of his style blind the reader to the fallacy of his criticism. The warrant for the existence of the Opera exists in the fact that the force of the words of the drama is added to, and accentuated, by the employment of the resources of a sister art. This was well put by the Abbé Du Bos in his *Réflexions critiques sur la Poésie et la Peinture* which appeared in 1719, a few years only after

Addison's essays. The work, often re-printed, was translated into English by Thomas Nugent (London, 1748 : 3 vols., 8vo). In the words of this translation, Music is " one of those means which have been invented in order to add a new strength to poetry, and to render it capable of making a greater impression." The discussion has been often revived, even in our own day, but no more need be said on the subject here.

Of the Liturgical dramas of the Middle Ages a full description, with examples, will be found in the *Drames liturgiques du Moyen Age* of Coussemaker (Paris, 1861 : 4to). But in point of fact the Modern Opera owes nothing to its religious proto-type. It was an entirely new departure, having its origin in the attempt of Vincenzo Galilei, Peri, and Caccini, with the help of the poet Rinuccini, to revive the ancient, and probably greatly overrated, glories of the Greek drama, an account of which will be found in every history of Music.

Considering that this attempt was made in Florence, and that after a few years Venice might almost be looked on as the headquarters of the Opera, it is remark-able how meagre the Italian literature of the subject is. We have the *Opera in Musica* of Antonio Planelli (Naples, 1772 :

8vo), a work which passes over the history
of the Opera very rapidly, and is devoted
rather to the æsthetic principles of the
subject, and to the means of putting them
into practice. A more important work
was *Le Rivoluzioni del Teatro Musicale
Italiano* of Stefano Arteaga (Bologna,
1783: 2 vols., 8vo; 2nd edition, Venice,
1785: 3 vols., 8vo), which received the
honours of translation into German at
the hands of Forkel (Leipzig, 1789: 8vo),
and of a French abridgment published
in London in 1802, octavo. The
work of Arteaga, who was a Spanish
Jesuit, is original and important, and
characterised by great clearness of judgment. We must also mention the little
work of that universal genius Count
Algarotti, *Saggio sopra l'Opera in Musica*,
the first edition ef which was published
in 1755, without name of place. It was
afterwards often reprinted, both alone and
in the collected editions of Algarotti's
works, and translated into English (London, 1767: 8vo; and Glasgow, 1768).
It is really a very sensible little book,
foreshadowing several of the views afterwards advocated by Gluck. If to these
works be added the brilliant little satire
of Benedetto Marcello—*Il Teatro alla
Moda*—first published without a date

(Borghi di Belisania [Venice] : 8vo), but probably in 1721, we have mentioned all the works of any importance which appeared in Italy before the present century. It professes to give instruction in their duties to all the various persons engaged in the Opera. It passed through several editions in Venice, and has been more than once reprinted during the present century—in one instance with the addition of a song in the Bolognese dialect in praise of Malibran !—and in a French translation by Ernest David (Paris, 1890 : 8vo).

It was in France that the greatest literary activity gathered around the Opera. Possessing no composer of the first rank, France has always attracted to its capital the most eminent operatic writers of other countries, and Paris has proved the battlefield of rival factions in the operatic world.

It is impossible to enter on this subject without some knowledge of the outlines of its history. Companies of Italian singers had been introduced into France by Mazarin to do pleasure to Anne of Austria. These performed exclusively at Court, where ballets had, for a long time, formed a favourite source of amusement, royal personages even not disdaining to take part in them. It was not till 1669 that Perrin obtained his patent for the establishment of a public theatre devoted to Opera, for which purpose he associated himself with Cambert as composer of the music. The arrangement was of short duration, for the wily Italian Lulli soon succeeded in ousting them, and in obtaining the patent for his exclusive advantage. The character of Lully, as his name became in France, was grasping and crafty, and he was very far from being loved. A satire directed against him appeared from the pen of La Fontaine, whom he employed as a librettist during the temporary disgrace of his favourite poet Quinault; but one of the most curious writings against him is the *Lettre de Clément Marot à Monsieur de . . . touchant ce qui s'est passé à l'arrivée de Jean Baptiste Lully aux Champs-Elysées* (Cologne [?], 1688: 12mo), by Antoine Bauderon, Sieur de Sénecé, whose grievance was of a like nature to La Fontaine's. The author does not scruple to accuse Lully of the actual murder of Cambert.

The reader will not need telling that the genius of Lully was in every way successful, and that he was adopted by the nation as the French composer. His claims and those of his successors were not, however, universally admitted. They were contested in a pamphlet by the Abbé Raguenet, who had travelled in Italy, entitled *Parallèle des Italiens et des Français, en ce qui regarde la Musique et les Opéras* (Paris, 1702: 12mo; English translation, London, 1709: 8vo). Such an indictment against the national taste could not go unanswered, and in 1704 Lecerf de la Vieville replied with much vigour in his *Comparaison de la Musique italienne et de la Musique françoise,* (Brussels, 1704: 12mo), and in the following year the work was reprinted, with additions, containing a life of Lully and a history of Music and the Opera. The work called forth a reply from Raguenet, with whom the honours of the controversy remained. The English translation of Raguenet's book, to which an interesting appendix on "Operas and Musick in England" is added, is attributed to Galliard by Hawkins, but this view is contested by Burney. Whoever is answerable for it, the English is very quaint and curious.

The controversy was allowed to slumber for the greater part of half a century, when an Italian company visited Paris and produced the delightful little duologue of Pergolesi, *La Serva Padrona*. This was the signal for the renewal of the conflict with increased bitterness. Then broke out the famous *Guerre des Bouffons*, in which every one who was a wit, or assumed to be one, was compelled to take sides, and to belong either to the " Coin du Roi," which supported the patriotic view, or the " Coin de la Reine," which declared for Italian music. Among the combatants were Grimm, D'Holbach, D'Alembert, Travenol, Cazotte, the Abbé Arnaud, Frederick the Great—and, hottest of all in the fray—J. J. Rousseau, who declared that " the French have no music, and never will have any ; and if they ever should have, it will be so much the worse for them " (*Lettre sur la Musique française*, 1753). Those who wish to investigate the subject for themselves will find a complete bibliography, carefully drawn up by E. Thoinan, in vol. ii. p. 449 of the supplement to the *Dictionnaire* of Fétis. But the controversy is dreary reading ! All the sparkle has long evaporated. The catalogue, as here given, comprises sixty-three works. Most of them are, of course, only pamphlets of a few pages, which get thrown away when read ; it is therefore very difficult—almost impossible—to form a complete collection. The writer, for many years past, has availed himself of every opportunity that offered, but has succeeded in

acquiring little more than half the series
—many more, however, than he has had
the patience to read!

The war came to an end from the
exhaustion of the combatants on either
side, the last stray shot being an article
inserted by D'Alembert in his well-known
Mélanges (1759). But the peace was
not destined to be a lasting one. In
1774, with the protection of Marie
Antoinette, Gluck produced his *Iphigénie
en Aulide* in Paris. Its success was
followed by that of *Orphée,, Alceste,* and
Armide. The advocates of Italian music,
annoyed at Gluck's triumph, brought
Piccinni to Paris. The war between the
advocates of the Austrian and of the
Italian broke out with a fierceness greater
even than that of the *Guerre des Bouffons.*
Marmontel, La Harpe, Ginguené, D'Alembert, Framéry, espoused the Italian cause,
Suard and the Abbé Arnaud that of
Gluck. The discussion was more sincere,
as it involved the defence of definite principles, and was not so obviously continued
simply to air the wit of the disputants
as was that of the *Guerre des Bouffons.*
Fortunately the principal contributions
to the discussion were collected in a
volume by the Abbé Leblond under the
title of *Mémoires pour servir à l'Histoire*

de la Révolution opérée dans la Musique par M. le Chevalier Gluck (Naples (?) and Paris, 1781 : 8vo), so that the course of the discussion can be readily followed. The advocates of Gluck had the good sense to base their arguments on the principles enunciated in Gluck's famous dedication to Maria Theresa of the opera *Alceste,* a translation of which appears in this collection, and has been quoted over and over again ; but it may be well to add that the original is to be found in the edition of the full score of the opera published in Vienna by Trattner in 1769. His views were further emphasized in the dedication of *Paride ed Elena* (Vienna, 1770), both of which original editions are far from common. The discussion was prolonged from the year 1772 to 1780, when more serious matters began to agitate the nation. The best works on the subject of Gluck and his influence are Anton Schmid's *Christopher Willibald Ritter von Gluck, dessen Leben und tonkunstlerisches Wirken* (Leipzig, 1854 : 8vo), a book abounding in detail and executed with great care ; and in French— *Gluck et Piccinni* 1774–1800—by G. Desnoiresterres (Paris, 1872 : 8vo), a book specially devoted to the considera- tion of Gluck's influence in France ; while

Mr. Ernest Newman has recently published a most painstaking work on the subject, under the title *Gluck and the Opera* : *a Study in Musical History* (London, 1895 : 8vo).

Turning now to works devoted to the history of the Opera in France, the earliest to be mentioned are the two little volumes of the learned Jesuit, Menestrier— *Des réprésentations en Musique anciennes et modernes* (Paris, 1681 : 12mo) and *Des ballets anciens et modernes selon les règles du Théâtre* (Paris, 1682 : 12mo), both forming parts of a larger work never carried out, and containing much information, the fruits of original research ; but their date covers but a very small portion of the history of the subject. The anonymous *Histoire du Théâtre de l'Opéra en France* (Paris, 1753 : 8vo) was by Jacques Durey de Noinville, assisted by Louis Travenol, a violinist in the opera band and one of those who joined in the *Guerre des Bouffons*, whose taste for literature led him into several scrapes. Little is to be said in favour of the book ; its interest lies in the information about the *personnel* of the Opera and in a chronological list of works produced.

The *Art du Théâtre* of Nougaret (Paris, 1769 : 2 vols., 12mo) contains information on the history of the Opera and of the Opera Comique ; while the anonymous *Histoire de l'Opéra Bouffon* (Paris, 1768 : 2 vols., 12mo), the author of which was Contant D'Orville, gives details both of the plot and caste of the works performed at that theatre ; the *Histoire du Théâtre de l'Opéra Comique* (Paris, 1769 : 2 vols., 12mo) follows the same course. The author of this work was J. A. Jullien, known under the name of Desboulmiers. *Les Trois Théâtres de Paris* of Des Essarts (Paris, 1777 : 8vo) gives a very rapid history of the Opera, but is mainly interesting from the fact that it contains all the *arrêts* governing the management of that theatre.

Covering a later period are the *Mémoires, ou essais sur la Musique* by the Citoyen Grétry (Paris, *Pluviose, an V.* [1797] : 3 vols., 8vo). The details are almost exclusively about his own operas, but the book is amusing reading. While Martine, in his *Musique dramatique en France* (Paris, 1813 : 8vo), gives many particulars about the operas of Grétry, Philidor, Monsigny, D'Alayrac, Boieldieu, Méhul, and other French composers of that time.

In 1820 Castil-Blaze, who was educated for the bar, and had become *sous-*

prefet in the department of Vaucluse,
threw up his appointment and came to
Paris, with a view of publishing his work,
De l'Opéra en France (Paris, 1820 : 2 vols.,
8vo). It was the most valuable work
which had appeared up to that time. It
is critical rather than historical, and the
title does not describe the full scope of
the book. The first volume is really an
introduction to the art, as opposed to
the science, of Music, and contains much
valuable advice on the choice of words,
the selection and training of voices, the
constitution of the orchestra, on accompaniment, etc., conveyed with great vigour
of language. The second volume considers in detail the various parts of an
opera, with a valuable chapter on the
history of Opera in the provinces. The
success of the work obtained for Castil-
Blaze the position of musical critic of the
Journal des Débats, and he became from
that time one of the most active writers
on music, although none of his subsequent
works are so valuable as that just noticed
—in fact, he became the facile musical
feuilletoniste, aiming at amusement rather
than instruction. He projected a series
of works on the lyric theatres of Paris, of
which there appeared *L'Académie Impériale
de Musique de* 1645 *à* 1855 (Paris, 1855 :

2 vols., 8vo) and *l'Opéra Italien de* 1548 *à* 1856 (Paris, 1856 : 1 vol., 8vo). In these works the author is disposed to run off into amusing gossip, not always very pertinent. Much of the information is taken from the immense MS. collections on the history of the Opera, both in France and in other countries, made by Beffara, *commissaire de police* in Paris from 1792 to 1816, forming eighty volumes, quarto and folio, of patient researches, which he left to the City of Paris, and which were disastrously burnt during the Commune. Castil-Blaze announced a work on the Opéra Comique, but did not live to publish it; the manuscript has been acquired by the Library of the Opera.

An excellent work on the Opera in France is M. Gustave Chouquet's *Histoire de la Musique Dramatique en France* (Paris, 1873 : 8vo), which covers the whole ground, and will be found useful. M. Pougin's *Vrais créateurs de l'Opera français* (Paris, 1881 : 12mo) is devoted to a detailed and interesting account of the ousting of Cambert and Perrin by Lully, while *Les origines de l'Opera français*, by Nuitter (the Archivist of the Opera) and Thoinan (Paris, 1886 : 8vo), although going over much of the same ground, contains useful information as to the position of the earlier homes of the Opera, a question also discussed in *Les treize salles de l'Opéra* of Lasalle (Paris, 1875 : 12mo).

Of modern operas, much criticism will be found in the republished collections of contributions to newspapers which are so common in France, while almost unknown in this country, such as those of Scudo, Adam, Berlioz, and others. Berlioz's own operas gave rise to much controversy. The Parisians at that time had not discovered the merits of Berlioz as a composer, and as a critic he had hit hard, so that there was no lack of those ready to retaliate, both in the press and in caricature. An amusing collection of the latter will be found in the *Hector Berlioz* of Adolphe Jullien (Paris, 1888 : 4to), who is also the author of several pamphlets on points of interest connected with the Opera.

But by far the most valuable work on the Opera in France is the admirable Catalogue of the Musical Library of the Opera, by M. Théodore de Lajarte, the excellent librarian of that establishment. In it may be traced the history of nearly all the operas which have been produced, form the time of Cambert to our own day. The catalogue is arranged chronologically, specifying what scores and parts of each opera exist in the library, the author of the music and words, the date of first representation, with the caste, and a mention of the various "numbers" which became celebrated. To these details are appended admirable notes, giving many interesting particulars of the different works, while short biographies are added of the authors both of the words and music. The work, which comes down to December 1876, is handsomely printed (Paris, Jouast, 1877 : 2 vols., 8vo), and illustrated by excellent etched portraits by Le Rat, and is furnished with necessary indexes—a merit not always possessed by French books.

Space is wanting to refer to the numerous biographies of eminent performers ; we may perhaps, however, mention two works on the witty and brilliant Sophie Arnould—*Arnoldiana, ou Sophie Arnould et ses contemperains* (Paris, 1813 : 12mo), and *Sophie Arnould*, by E. and J. de Goncourt (Paris, 1857 : 12mo), and these lead us to speak of Campardon's *L'Académie Royale de Musique au XVIIIe. siècle—Documents inédits découverts aux Archives nationales* (Paris, 1884 : 8vo), two handsome volumes, consisting of a dictionary, mainl devoted to all those connected with that theatre who had the misfortune to be concerned in any legal process, with particulars and documents, which it may well be supposed are frequently of a very edifying nature. An attempt is made to give a list of all the parts which each performer undertook, so that the book is not wholly useless. Finally we should mention M. E. G. J. Gregoir's *Des Gloires de l'Opéra et la Musique à Paris* (Brussels, 1878-81 : 3 vols., 8vo), which we believe is all that has been published, although the work is not complete. It consists of a very remarkable collection of facts and documents connected with the Opera in France, set down in an order roughly chronological, but entirely deficient in arrangement, with the usual absence of index, which, in such a work, is of the first importance.

The history of the Opera in France was identical with the history of the Opera in Paris. In Germany there were many centres of musical activity at the various Courts which maintained a theatre. There is no doubt that Hamburg was the first place where this form of amusement took any hold of the public, and that this result was mainly owing to Reinhold Keiser. All the contemporary information we have about him is to be found in the *Ehrenpforte* of Mattheson, for Walther, in his dictionary, adds nothing to the particulars there given, for which he acknowledges his indebtedness to Mattheson, who, from his continued residence in Hamburg and his personal connexion with that theatre, had the best opportunities of acquiring them. The early history of the German Opera has been investigated by Dr. E. O. Lindner in his *Die erste stehende Deutsche Oper* (Berlin, 1855 : 8vo), who has added, in a separate volume, a series of extracts from the exceedingly rare works of Keiser. H. M. Schletterer has traced the history of the German "Singspiel"—*i.e.*, a piece in which singing alternates with spoken dialogue—in his *Das deutsche Singspiel von seinem ersten Aufängen bis auf die neueste Zeit* (Augsburg, 1863 : 8vo).

The rest of the German literature on the Opera (with the exception of that on Wagner) mainly resolves itself into records of the work carried on at the principal theatres, with the *personnel* of the staff. The proceedings of the Opera in nearly all the larger cities are thus recorded. Of Berlin we have L. Schneider's *Geschichte der Oper und des Königlichen Opernhauses* (Berlin, 1852 : 8vo), and more recently Brachvogel's *Geschichte des*

Königlichen Theaters zu Berlin (Berlin 1877-8 : 2 vols., 8vo), the second volume of which is devoted to the Opera. Dresden is also rich in such works. We have M. Fürstenau's *Zur Geschichte der Musik und des Theaters am Hofe zu Dresden* (Dresden, 1861, 1862 : 2 vols., 8vo), an interesting book which, however, carries us no further than 1763, and Prölss's *Geschichte des Hoftheaters zu Dresden von seinen Aufängen bis zum Jahre* 1862 (Dresden, 1878 : 8vo), furnished with excellent tables of the works performed and of the artists engaged. The history of the Opera in Dresden is interesting from the fact that Weber was for a time music-director there, fighting the battle of national opera against Italian, which was then in universal favour. Darmstadt has an excellent record in H. Knispel's *Das Grossherzogliche Hoftheater in Darmstadt von* 1810—1890 (Darmstadt, 1891 : large 8vo), a work with a first-rate index —so rare a merit in German books that it ought to be mentioned. Leipzig has found chroniclers both in Kneschke—*Zur Geschichte des Theaters und der Musik in Leipzig* (Leipzig, 1864 : 8vo)—and in Müller—*Das Stadt-Theater Leipzig* (*ib.*, 1891 : 8vo) ; and several other towns have records of a like nature. If Weimar possesses any such history, the writer is ignorant of it. It would be of great interest, on account of the work carried on there by Liszt during the time he was conductor of the Court theatre. Much information on the period is to be found in Liszt's Correspondence, recently edited by La Mara (Leipzig, 1893 : 2 vols., 8vo), which has been excellently translated by Miss Constance Bache (London, 1894 : 2 vols., 8vo), as well as in the correspondence of Wagner, which was also rendered into English by the late Dr. Hueffer (London, 1888 : 2 vols., 8vo), and a further series by Mr. Shedlock (London, 1890 : 8vo).

These works lead us to speak of the overwhelming amount of literature which Wagner's theories of Art have called forth. Without giving details of the original and separate editions of his literary works, it may be noted that they were collected in ten volumes octavo (Leipzig, 1871-85), and in a cheaper reprint (Leipzig, 1887-8: 10 vols., 8vo). The *Guerre des Bouffons* and the Gluck and Piccinni contest sink into insignificance by the side of the vast mass of literature which has collected and is still collecting round his name. Herr Oseterlein has made a catologue of his own enormous collection, which in itself fills three large octavo volumes, running to 9462 items, and a supplementary volume has just appeared. This vast number includes portraits of the composer and of those who assisted in the performance of his works or were otherwise concerned in the movement, as well as newspaper notices. Nothing seems to have escaped the grasp of this indefatigable collector.

The best account of Wagner's life and works is to be found in Glasenapp's *Richard Wagner's Leben und Wirken* (1st edition, Leipzig, 1876–7 : 2 vols., 8vo ; 2nd edition, *ib.*, 1882. A third is in course of publication). The same writer has compiled a *Wagner Lexicon* (Stuttgart, 1883 : 8vo)—a useful exposition of "the Master's" views. There exists also another curious little dictionary about Wagner by Tappert—of all the impolite things which have been said of him by his opponents—*Wörterbuch der Unhöflichkeit . . . gegen den Meister* (Leipzig, 1877 : 8vo).

In France, one of the most serious works in advocacy of his theories is *Le Drame musicale* of E. Schuré (Paris, 1875 : 2 vols., 8vo), but in that country the question has been greatly prejudiced by political views, while caricature, on the whole good-natured, has had free scope.

Many of these, with much other interesting matter, and numerous portraits, have been collected in the handsome volume of Adolphe Jullien—*Richard Wagner, sa vie, et ses œuvres* (Paris, 1886 : 4to)—a companion volume to the same writer's *Berlioz*, already spoken of. An equally amusing volume, of more modest proportions, is *Richard Wagner en caricatures*, by John Grand-Carteret (Paris [1893] : 8vo). The French are admirable in the compilation of such books.

In England, one of Wagner's warmest advocates was the late Dr. Hueffer. His *Richard Wagner and the Music of the Future* (London, 1874 : 8vo), as well as his little book, *Richard Wagner* (London, 1881 : 8vo), one of the " Great Musicians " series, may be read with advantage. Mr. Dannreuther has translated several of Wagner's works into English, including *The Music of the Future, Beethoven*, and *On Conducting*, while Mr. Ashton Ellis has begun the Herculean task of translating the whole of the works into English. Three volumes have already appeared, executed with most painstaking care.

The writer has not succeeded in finding any work embracing the history of Opera in Vienna, but Von Köchel's excellent *Johann Josef Fux* (Vienna, 1872 : 8vo) furnishes much information of its early days, giving a list of all the works produced from 1631 to 1740, a catalogue greatly added to by Pohl in his *Josef Haydn*, already referred to. Of late (possibly for many years past) a *Jahrbuch des Hof Operntheaters* is published.

Of most of the Italian opera-houses, statements of the works performed have been published from time to time, such as that of La Scala at Milan by Romani (Milan, 1862 : 4to), many of the smaller towns even adopting this excellent habit. In Venice, the cradle of the Opera, a work of this nature was published as early as 1730, entitled *Le Glorie della Poesia e della Musica* (Venice : 12mo). This is said to be by J. C. Bonlini. It covers a very interesting period, is arranged chronologically, in many cases interesting notices of the works are added, and there is an excellent index. A *Catalogo di tutti i Drammi per Musica*, bringing the list down to 1745, was produced in that year, "posto in luce," by Antonio Groppo, who stands on the title as its printer. The printer of the earlier work, according to the privilege, was Bonarigo. The type of both works appears to be identical, the dedication to the reader is in absolutely the same words, and it is difficult to believe that they have not a common origin. The notices are omitted in Groppo.

In our own country we are badly provided with records of our opera-houses —in fact, no systematic works of this nature exist. For the early history of the subject, and for details of the operas produced by Handel and others, the *History* of Burney is the best authority, and it is mainly from this source that Hogarth and Sutherland Edwards have derived their information. Some particulars of a later period may be found in the Earl of Mount Edgcumbe's *Musical Reminiscences* (1st edition, London, 1825 ; the 4th and most recent, London, 1834 : 12mo), and also in the amusing and gossiping *Reminiscences* of Michael Kelly (London, 1826 : 2 vols., 8vo) and in the *Musical Memoirs* of W. T. Parke, the oboe player (London, 1830 : 2 vols., 8vo) ; but both these works must be used with caution. The former contains an appendix on the history of the King's Theatre in the Haymarket. *Seven years of the King's Theatre*, by John Ebers (London, 1828 : 8vo), a librarian who was induced to become lessee of that house, is a more systematic record from 1821 to 1827 of the history of Opera during that period, and gives an excellent idea of the vicissitudes of a manager's career. The *Reminiscences* of Benjamin Lumley, another equally unsuccessful manager, cover the history of the same house from 1841 to 1858, while *The Mapleson Memoirs*, 1848—1888 (London, 1888 : 2 vols., 8vo), come down to the final closing of the theatre. It will be seen that of the latter years of the enterprise we possess something like a connected series, although amounting to little more than gossip. Of the course of events at that admirably appointed house, Covent Garden, during the rule of the late Mr. Gye, we unfortunately possess no chronicle ; Mr. Gruneisen has, however, put on record the circumstances which led to its establishment.

We conclude this chapter by directing attention to certain works of the greatest utility to all who have occasion to study the history of the Opera. Of these, the well-known *Drammaturgia* of Lione Allacci is the prototype. The best edition is that of Venice, 1755, 4to. It consists of an alphabetical dictionary of all the dramatic works, including operas, which had been produced in Italy up to that date. Still more useful in our own day is the *Dictionnaire Lyrique* of

F. Clément and Larousse (Paris, *s.a.* :
8vo), which, apart from some of the
faults inevitable in such an undertaking,
the writer has found most helpful.   The
compilers have added many interesting
details as to the success of the different
works, with particulars of the most popular
numbers—in fact, just the information
which one wants.   The drawback of such
a work is that the lapse of time renders
supplements necessary, several of which
we believe have already been added.
A similar work in German by Dr.
Riemann, under the title of *Opern
Handbuch* (Leipzig, 1887), has been published.   Less detail is entered into, but
the book has the advantage that the
names of composers are inserted in their
alphabetical position, with a list of their
works, which adds to its convenience as
a book of reference.   A tolerably bulky
supplement forms part of the volume as
originally published.

CHAPTER X.

THE LITERATURE OF MUSICAL
INSTRUMENTS.

THE origin and development of the various instruments of music cannot fail to be a subject of interest to the musician. The invention of many of them is lost in antiquity. The earliest printed work on the subject is the *Musica getutscht* of Sebastian Virdung, which is supposed to have been printed at Basle in 1511 (obl. 4to). The book, which is in German, is in the form of a dialogue, and contains descriptions, with woodcuts, of all the instruments then existing, including both the clavichord and the virginal, with keyboards as at present in use. The book is of the greatest rarity, five copies only being known, of which one is in the possession of Mr. Alfred Littleton, and another of the writer. Fortunately an admirable facsimile was issued by the Gesellschaft für Musikforschung, which, for all practical purposes, is as useful as the original. The *Musurgia* of Ottomar Luscinius (Nachtigall) (Strasburg, 1536: obl. 4to) is little more than a translation into Latin, with additions, of the treatise of Virdung, and the identical wood blocks are used. Another early work of interest, also with woodcuts, is the *Musica instrumentalis deudsch* of Martin Agricola (Wittemberg, 1528 : 8vo), more than once reprinted. We have already described at some length the *Syntagma* of Michael Prætorius. The *Theatrum Instrumentorum*, forming part of this work (Wolfenbüttel, 1620 : 4to), gives interesting illustrations of the instruments of a later date. Fortunately this part of the work has been reproduced.

Coming to the instruments of the modern orchestra, those of the violin family claim the first notice. So admirable a bibliography of the subject has just been completed by Mr. E. Heron-Allen, under the title of *De Fidiculis Bibliographia* (London, 1890-94 : 2 vols., 4to), that we might almost content ourselves with directing our readers to that work; there are, however, a few prominent works which ought to be mentioned.

Books on the violin (which must here

be understood to include the viola, violoncello, and contrabasso), which give an account of the different makers, and attempt to distinguish their different characteristics, have a perennial interest for all owners of such instruments. The most important of these is the *Instruments à archet* of Antoine Vidal (Paris, 1876-78 : 3 vols., 4to), printed in sumptuous style, with numerous etchings by F. Hillemacher. The first volume, after tracing the early history of the violin, gives an account of the rise of the great schools of violin-making, followed by lists of the workers in Italy, Germany, Holland, Belgium, England, and France, amply illustrated by well-executed facsimiles of the tickets they used. The volume concludes with an account of the principal bow-makers.

The second volume considers at some length the interesting questions of the *Roi des Violons*, and the *Corporation des Menestriers*. This is followed by a history of the art of violin-playing, with notices, and in many cases portraits, of the most celebrated violinists and violoncellists. Vol. iii. is occupied with biographies of composers of chamber-music, to which is appended an excellent bibliography of music of that nature.

The work is turned out with true

French splendour, so that its money value is considerable. To suit purchasers anxious to possess the part of the work relating to the different makers and their instruments, M. Vidal was induced to issue it in large octavo form in 1889, under the title *La Lutherie et les Luthiers.* In it he availed himself of the latest knowledge ; the etched copies of tickets are replaced by photogravures, which are even more successful.

Another sumptuous little book is *Les Luthiers Italiens*, of M. Jules Gallay (Paris, Académie de Bibliophiles, 1869 : 8vo). In the year 1806 the Abbé Sibire issued a book on the Italian makers, under the title of *La Chélomanie* (Paris : 8vo), from information supplied to him by the well-known maker, Lupot. The work, and a second edition (Brussels, 1823 : 12mo), both became exceedingly rare. It is a reprint of this work which forms the principal part of M. Gallay's book, but its value is enhanced by much valuable information, supplied by the editor. Strange to say, this book, in its turn, has become exceedingly scarce. An inferior reprint of *La Chélomanie* has been made at Brussels, 1885 : 12mo.

In English we have Sandys' and Forster's *History of the Violin* (London,

1864 : 8vo), a work of considerable value, travelling over the whole subject, but of special interest as regards our English workmen. One of the authors was a member of the well-known Forster family, who obtained such deserved reputation, especially for their violoncellos; the family is, therefore, treated with great detail. Much information will also be found as to the introduction of many of Haydn's works to the English public, William Forster " No. 1 " having acquired the copyright of them in this country.

Another English violin-maker—George Hart—has also published a work which has attained to considerable popularity— *The Violin ; its Famous Makers and Their Imitators* (London, 1875 : 4to ; and also a cheaper edition, 8vo). The great experience which the author had, as a dealer, renders his opinions valuable, and the work is illustrated by woodcuts of instruments, which are as excellent as it is possible to be. It has been translated into French by A. Royer (Paris, 1886 : 4to). Mr. Hart published a further work, called *The Violin and its Music* (London, 1881 : 4to and 8vo), illustrated with steel portraits of eminent violinists, but the book is of less interest than the preceding volume.

Books of less pretention, but still valuable, are J. M. Fleming's *Old Violins and Their Makers* (London, 1883 : 8vo ; and certainly one subsequent edition), Joseph Pearce's *Violins and Violin Makers* (London, 1866 : 8vo), while those who wish to try their hand at the difficult art of violin-making will find all the information which a book can impart in the excellent and clearly written *Violin Making as it was and is* (London, 1884 : 8vo ; with a second edition in 1885, and subsequent reprints), by Mr. E. Heron-Allen, who writes from practical acquaintance with the subject. There is also an excellent little handbook of the art in the Roret Manuals, by Mangin and Maigne (Paris, 1869 : 12mo (2nd edition). A very popular book also has been Otto's *On the Violin*, of which there are three German editions. The best English translation is that of Mr. John Bishop, whose notes add greatly to its value.

In Italian we have the *Liutai Antichi e Moderni* of Giovanni de Piccolellis (Florence, 1885 : large 8vo), an excellent work, illustrated with photogravures of a number of fine specimens. A supplementary note to this work was published in 1886. Germany has given us the painstaking and exhaustive *Geschichte der Bogen In-*

strumente of Julius Rühlmann (Brunswick,
1882 : 8vo ; with an atlas of plates, obl.
4to), a book to be strongly recommended
as trustworthy. Mr. Heron-Allen tells us
the remarkable circumstance that the
author was not a violinist, but a trumpet-
player !

The acoustic principles of the violin
were first scientifically investigated by
Félix Savart in a *Mémoire sur la construction des Instrumens à Cordes et à Archet*,
read before the Académie des Sciences
on May 31st, 1819. It is in this paper
that Savart's famous box violin is described. It was referred to a mixed
committee of musicians and scientific
men, including Cherubini and Biot, who
drew up an elaborate report. No doubt
this is to be found in the proceedings of
the Académie, but both the paper and the
report were printed as an octavo pamphlet
(Paris, 1819), by the author. In neither
of these forms is it very accessible, but,
as every book on the violin refers to these
researches, the reader may be glad to
know that there is a German translation
(Leipzig, 1844 : 8vo), while an English
version is to be found in Davidson's *The
Violin* (London, 1881 : 8vo [the 4th
edition]).

In addition to these general works on

the subject, there are certain monographs which should be mentioned. Among these is Fétis's *Antoine Stradivari* (Paris, 1856 : 8vo) which, however, is more comprehensive than its title suggests. In 1891 Messrs. W. E. Hill & Sons, the well-known and respected makers, issued two most sumptuous little works, one on the famous Stradiuarius known as " *Le Messie*," the other on the " Tuscan " Stradiuarius— each of them illustrated with chromolithographs by Mr. Alfred Slocombe, which are the most wonderful representations of violins ever executed ; while in 1892 they produced a work of even greater value by Mrs. Huggins, on the Life and Work of G. P. Maggini, illustrated with equal skill by the same artist. Messrs. Hill have a work on Stradivari in progress.

The early history of the violin, and its development, have been well treated by the late Carl Engel in his *Researches into the Early History of the Violin Family* (London: 8vo), a posthumous work, issued under the editorship of Mr. Hipkins. It shows all the careful investigation for which that excellent student of the development of musical instruments was well known ; and we should mention J. W. von Wasielewski's *Die Violine und ihre Meister* (Leipzig, 1869 : 8vo ; enlarged editions 1883, and 1893), which passes in review nearly all the violinists known to fame, while his *Das Violoncell und seine Geschichte* (Leipzig, 1889 : 8vo) performs the same office for the violoncello. The latter work has been translated into English by Miss Stigand (London, 1894 : 8vo). The well-known book, *Dubourg on the Violin,* consists mainly of an amusing collection of anecdotes and gossip, more or less anthentic.

The violin and its fellows did not achieve their proud position without a struggle with their predecessors, the fretted viols. This found its expression in a rare little work, the *Défense de la Basse de Viole contre les Entreprises du Violon et les Prétentions du Violoncel. Par Monsieur Hubert Le Blanc, Docteur en Droit* (Amsterdam, 1740 : 12mo). The book, although small, is tedious ; its principal value rests in the information it gives about the French viol players, and especially about Marin Marais. Another rare book on the viol must also be mentioned, the *Traité de la Viole* of Jean Rousseau (Paris, 1687 : 8vo), which also contains, in the introduction, some interesting details about French performers on the instrument.

The wind instruments of the orchestra have made little mark in literature, with the exception of the flute. The scale of the old eight-key flute was both out of tune and uneven in quality and power, and it was not until the improvements of Boehm that this instrument became tolerable. Boehm's inventions were claimed for Captain Gordon, a Swiss of English origin, who was an officer in the French Royal Guard. The first note of the controversy was sounded in 1838 by M. Coche, professor at the Paris Conservatoire, who published a pamphlet, *Examen critique de la Flûte ordinaire comparée à la Flûte de Böhm*, which was mainly designed to recommend a flute, with still further improvements, by the writer. In this he had many imitators, who, while producing pamphlets in praise of their own particular adaptation of them, all base them on Boehm's—or Gordon's—inventions. In 1881 Boehm died, at an advanced age, and the discussion was revived. In the following year Mr. W. S. Broadwood published an original "essay" by Boehm "on the construction of the flute," which had remained in manuscript since 1847, "with correspondence and other documents" (London, 1882 : 8vo), in which the scientific principles involved are investigated, while in 1883 Mr. C. Welch brought out his *History of the Boehm Flute*, in which the controversy is treated in a judicial spirit, so that the reader who is interested in the subject may be safely guided by it.

Considering the popularity of the " household orchestra," it is remarkable how little has been written about the pianoforte in England, apart from mere advertisements of particular makers. *The Pianoforte, its Origin, Progress, and Construction* of the late Dr. Rimbault (London, 1860 : 4to) is somewhat inadequate. The best sources of information are the articles on the pianoforte and its predecessors by Mr. A. J. Hipkins, to be found in Grove's *Dictionary*, in which both the history and the mechanism are treated with perfect knowledge. An excellent summary, fully establishing the claims of Cristofori to the invention of the pianoforte, will be found in the *Cenni storici . . . della origine del Pianoforte*—a paper read to the Reale Istituto Musicale of Florence in 1873 by Cav°. Puliti, but published separately in 1874, which contains excellent diagrams of the actions invented by Cristofori, as well as of those contrived by Marius of Paris, and by Schrœter, a German, for both of whom the invention has been claimed. The latter was a musician, and not a maker of instruments, and it is asserted that his ideas were put into practical form by the famous Silbermann. Schrœter's claims are warmly advocated by Dr. Oscar Paul in his *Geschichte des Klaviers* (Leipzig, 1868 : 8vo). The placing of a tablet to the memory of Cristofori in the Church of Santa Croce in 1876 formed the occasion of a little work by C. Ponsicchi, *Il Pianoforte sua origine e sviluppo* (Firenze, 1876 : 8vo), with diagrams. *Der Flügel* of H. Welcker von Gontershausen (Frankfort-on-Main, 1856 : 4to), *Der Clavierbau,* of the same author (*ib.*, 1870 : 8vo), and *Il Pianoforte* by G. F. Sievers (Naples, 1868 : large 8vo), aim at being practical guides to the art of constructing piano-fortes. They are both amply illustrated with diagrams. There is also an excellent little *Manuel complet de l'accordeur et du réparateur de Pianos* by G. Huberson in the Roret series (Paris, 1891 : 12mo) ; while the *Art d'accorder soi-même son piano,* by the very remarkable blind piano-manu-facturer, Claude Montal, the editions and translations of which are numerous, may be useful to those who find themselves far removed from a tuner.

We may here mention the *Geschichte des*

Clavierspiels of the late C. F. Weitzmann (Stuttgart, 1863 : 8vo), an excellent history, with examples, of the development of the art.

The literature of the organ is very extensive. The first work we have to mention is one of great excellence, and also of great splendour—*L'Art du Facteur d'Orgues*, by Dom Bedos de Celles, a Benedictine of St. Maur, which forms part of the Encyclopédie des Arts et Métiers (Paris, 1766 : 2 vols., large folio). The first volume contains the text, while the second is devoted to the plates. It is impossible to speak too highly of this admirable work, and the plates are truly magnificent. Every detail of the organ is accurately figured, and every tool used is represented. Some of the plates are on a very large scale, that of the organ at Weingarten, for instance, measuring twenty-seven by twenty and a half inches, exclusive of margin, while the representation of the interior of an organ is thirty inches by twenty-four. They are all engraved in the highest style of art, and it is a real pleasure to examine them. The book is by no means uncommon, and should be in the possession of every one interested in the " king of instruments."

The Roret cyclopædia contains a *Nouveau Manuel complet du Facteur d'Orgues* by M. Hamel, based on the previous work, comprised in three 12mo volumes of text, and a folio atlas of plates (Paris, 1849). The work is brought to a more modern standard, and is an excellent little book. The plates are clear and adequate, but of course very far from reproducing the splendour of the original work.

In our own language we are fortunate in possessing a treatise of great excellence —*The Organ* of Dr. Rimbault and Mr. E. Hopkins (London, 1855, and two subsequent editions : large 8vo). The historical part, by Dr. Rimbault, is fairly done, but the technical part, by Mr. Hopkins, is a model. The author has very exceptional skill in describing mechanism, which makes the book a delight to all who are interested in the subject. The writer is glad to record his personal gratitude for the pleasure and instruction he has derived from it.

Till the production of this book, as far as the writer knows, the only work in the English language on the subject was a translation of Seidel on the organ (London, 1855 [2nd edition] : 8vo). The work is a curiosity, for the translator apparently knew nothing of the organ, and but little of the language into which he was endeavouring to turn the original. Seidel was an organist at Breslau, and if the translation were only intelligible, it would not be a bad book; as it stands it becomes amusing to those who can fathom the author's meaning.

The success attained to by the earlier organ-builders was the result of experience. The first to apply scientific and mathematical knowledge to the subject was Gottlob Töpfer, an organist at Weimar. His *Orgelbau-Kunst nach einer neuen Theorie dargestellt* (Weimar, 1833: 8vo), with a supplement, forms an era in the art of organ-building, and has been the text-book for all who were not content with "rule of thumb." Töpfer published a second work — *Die Orgel, Zweck und Beschaffenheit ihre Theile,* etc. (Erfurt, 1843: 8vo). The late Aristide Cavaillé-Coll, the famous French organ-builder, was also a man of science, and the author, among other papers of *Études experimentales sur les tuyaux d'orgues,* read at the Académie in February 1849.

Of other practical works on organ-building, the earlier practice will be found well illustrated in the *Musica Mechanica Organoedi* of Jakob Adlung (Berlin, 1768 :

2 vols., 4to). *De Orgelmaaker* of J. van
Heurn (Dordrecht, 1805 : 3 vols., 8vo; with
an atlas of plates) is apparently an excellent work, with the disadvantage of being in
the Dutch language. To the numerous
class of amateurs who attempt organ-building, *Practical Organ-building*, by the Rev.
W. E. Dickson, Precentor of Ely, will
prove an excellent guide ; while in *Organs
and Organ-Building* (London, 1881 : 8vo)
much useful information will be found on
the developments of the pneumatic action
invented by our countryman Barker, which
have so revolutionised the interior of the
modern organ. It is a really excellent
little book. Some good hints as to organs
in small churches will be found in
Scudamore Organs, by the Rev. J. Baron,
which contains some excellent designs
for chancel organs by the late G. E.
Street (London, 1858 : 8vo).

The avidity with which lovers of the
organ collect specifications of these instruments is a recognised weakness, well
provided for among the works already
mentioned, especially in " Rimbault and
Hopkins," while the original specifications
of many organs which have been since
modified will be found in the anonymous *Sammlung einiger Nachrichten von
berühmten Orgel-Wercken in Teutschland*

(Breslau, 1757 : 4to), and of the famous Dutch organs in the *Dispositien der merk-waardigste Kerk-Orgelen* of Joachim Hess (Gouda, 1774; 4to); while nearly every church organ of any pretention on the Continent has been described in a pamphlet by the organist in office at the time of its erection. These, of course, it is impossible to enumerate.

In addition to the history of the organ by the late Dr. Rimbault, that industrious antiquary published a lecture on *The Early English Organ Builders and their works, from the Fifteenth Century to the period of the Great Rebellion* (London, 1865 : 8vo); there is also a charming little volume (by the late Sir John Sutton (?)), *A Short account of Organs built in England from the reign of King Charles the Second to the present Time* (London, 1847 : 8vo), while the famous strife between the rival builders, Father Smith and Renatus Harris is well chronicled in *A few notes on the Temple Organ,* by E. Macrory (London, *s.a.*: 8vo), which also describes Smith's method of introducing two extra notes in the octave. Much information on organs and organists in Belgium will be found in the *Historique de la Facture et des Facteurs d'Orgue* of E. G. J. Gregoir (Antwerp, 1865 : 8vo).

It may be a question whether the design of the case of an organ does not more properly belong to the literature of architecture than to that of Music, but the works we are proposing to mention contain so much other information that we must include them. The first of these is *Church Organs ; their position and construction. With an Appendix containing some account of the Mediæval Organ Case still existing at Old Radnor, South Wales* (London, 1872 : folio), by the Rev. F. H. Sutton, containing some admirable designs. *The Box of Whistles : an illustrated book on Organ Cases* (London, 1878 : folio) contains a large number of drawings of organs, both at home and abroad, executed with fair success in chromolithography after the drawings of the author, Mr. John Norbury, an accomplished amateur. *The Organ Cases and Organs of the Middle Ages and Renaissance,* by Mr. A. G. Hill, M.A., F.S.A., a member of the well-known and respected family of organ-builders (London, 1883, 1891 : 2 vols, large folio) is a really monumental work, containing seventy-five excellent lithographic facsimiles of the author's own drawings. The specification of the organ is in most cases given, and many historical and other useful notes are added, making it a work of great value and interest.

Mr. J. W. Warman began, in the *English Mechanic*, a series of elaborate articles on the construction of the organ, which were never brought to a conclusion, being probably on too detailed a scale for such a publication. Part of his proposed work has been published in a separate form, under the title of *The Organ ; its compass, tablature, and short and incomplete octaves* (London, 1884: 8vo). It contains exhaustive information on the subjects indicated—although it may be well to point out that by " tablature " Mr. Warman does not mean the peculiar method of notation for the organ which was made use of in old time. Mr. Warman is still labouring at his work, which is to contain a bibliography compiled with all possible completeness.

Zur Geschichte des Orgelspiels, vornehmlich des deutschen im 14 *bis zum Aufange des* 18 *Jahrhunderts* of A. G. Ritter (Leipzig, 1884: 2 vols., large 8vo) will be found a useful work on the subject of the early organ-players. The second volume contains examples of their works not otherwise easy of access. We must conclude this long notice of works on the organ by mentioning a useful little work on the law as affecting church organists—*The*

Law of Organs and Organists—by Blew (London, 1878 : 8vo)—an acquaintance with which both by the clergy and organists would avoid many unpleasant disputes. The book is additionally useful as it has an appendix on the " hire purchase " system—also a fruitful source of misunderstanding.

The modern harp owes its existence to the ingenuity of the late Sebastian Erard, whose inventions are recorded by Fétis in a *Notice Biographique* (Paris, 1831 : 4to). The article in the *Dictionnaire* of Fétis was also separately struck off as a pamphlet ; but the best description of the double-action harp, with excellent diagrams of its very ingenious mechanism, will be found in the Reports of the Exposition of 1855 (Paris, 1855 : 4to). It will suffice to mention Gunn's *Historical Enquiry respecting the performance of the Harp in the Highlands of Scotland* (Edinburgh, 1807 : 4to).

The inventive genius of the late Adolphe Sax (his real name was *Antoine Joseph Sax*) has revolutionised nearly the whole family of brass instruments. An interesting account of these will be found in Comettant's somewhat too extensive *Histoire d'un inventeur au XIXme. Siècle* (Paris, 1860 : 8vo).

Among the most interesting documents in connexion with musical instruments will be found the catalogues of collections of instruments, either in museums, or in specially organised exhibitions. Among these, our own collection at the South Kensington Museum is one of the best, and it is certainly the best catalogued. An excellent *Descriptive Catalogue*, containing an immense amount of information, was compiled by the late C. Engel, illustrated with photographs and cuts (London, 1874 : 8vo [2nd edition]) ; and there is a smaller catalogue of a more popular nature (London, [1875]: 8vo) by the same. A set of photographs of some of the principal objects, on a larger scale, was also issued by the Arundel Society, with an introduction and descriptions by the same writer (London, 1869 : folio).

The Museum of the Conservatoire at Paris is also an excellent collection, and has been catalogued by M. Gustave Chouquet. Two editions have been published (Paris, 1875 : 8vo ; and 1884 : 8vo), the latter with some illustrations. A supplement (1894) has already been found necessary. The Conservatoire at Brussels can also boast of a good collection, which has been catalogued by M. Mahillon.

An excellent loan exhibition was held

in the South Kensington Museum in 1872, the catalogue of which, enriched with photographs, had also the advantage of the able editing of Mr. Engel. A still finer collection was got together in connexion with the Inventions Exhibition in 1885—probably the most remarkable and most valuable assemblage ever united in one building. No attempt was made by the authorities to compile a catalogue worthy of so great an opportunity, the only one issued being a mere inventory, apparently drawn up by a clerk. Owing to private enterprise, the opportunity was not suffered to pass without a record— and a noble one—in the magnificent volume, *Musical Instruments, Historic, Rare, and Unique* (London, 1888 : folio), by Mr. A. J. Hipkins, whose name is sufficient guarantee of the excellence of the work ; but the author was fortunate in finding in Mr. William Gibb an artist who has a real genius for depicting such objects, and chromolithographers in Messrs. M'Lagan and Cuming, of Edinburgh, with skill to reproduce these drawings in a manner perfectly surprising. The work is a credit to every one concerned in its production.

A collection of military instruments formed part of the Military Exhibition of

1890. These found a most able cataloguer in Captain C. R. Day; the work (London, 1891 : 4to), while answering to its description as a catalogue, is really an excellent treatise on the construction and history of the different instruments used in military bands, and is illustrated both with woodcuts and with photogravures. To it is added an appendix on Musical Pitch, by Mr. D. J. Blaikley. While on the subject of military music, we may mention the *Manuel Général de Musique Militaire à l'usage des Armées Françaises*, by the late George Kastner (Paris, 1848 : 4to), which contains an interesting history of martial music among different nations, with descriptions of the instruments then in use, including those invented by Adolphe Sax.

Of private collections, the one that has been favoured with the most sumptuous catalogue is, without doubt, that of Mrs. J. Crosby Brown, of New York. It forms a large quarto volume, entitled *Musical Instruments and their Homes*, by Mary E. Brown, and William Adams Brown (New York, 1885). It is illustrated by a large number of facsimiles of pen-and-ink drawings of the various instruments, by W. Adams Brown. Much more modest is the catalogue of the *Musée Kraus* at

Florence (Florence, 1878 : 8vo), which is little more than a hand list, useful only in connexion with the specimens; but the Japanese instruments in the collection have a separate catalogue, *La Musique en Japon* (Florence, 1878 : 8vo), illustrated with numerous photographs. Japanese instruments are further treated of in *The Music and Musical Instruments of Japan*, by F. T. Piggott, with notes by T. L. Southgate—an excellent book, adequately illustrated. The visit of the Siamese military band to this country drew forth a small work, *Notes on Siamese Musical Instruments* (London, 1885 : 8vo), apparently well executed.

Raja Sir Sourindro Mohun Tagore, Mus. Doc., the most prominent of modern Hindu musicians, and a voluminous writer on the subject, has given us, *Yantra Kosha ; or a treasury of the musical instruments of Ancient and of Modern India* (Calcutta, 1875 : 8vo); but as the work is principally written in Hindustani, the writer is compelled to take its merits, which are no doubt great, on trust. In deference, however, to those who are debarred by this difficulty, the author has issued *Short Notices of Hindu Musical Instruments* (Calcutta, 1877), a funny little book measuring 4 in. × 3 in. For the finest work on Indian instruments we have again to thank both Captain C. R. Day for *The Music and Musical Instruments of Southern India and the Deccan*, and Mr. Gibb for the admirable illustrations (London, 1891 : 4to)—a beautiful book, most tastefully produced by Messrs. Novello & Co.

A comprehensive account of the practical construction of musical instruments of all kinds, from the Jew's-harp to the organ, will be found in H. Welcker von Gontershausen's *Neue eröffnetes Magazin Musicalischer Tonwerkzeuge* (Frankfort-on-Main, 1855 : 8vo), with numerous woodcuts. The *Organographie* of Comte de Pontécoulant (Paris, 1861 : 2 vols., 8vo), a somewhat discursive book, with a similar purpose, contains much interesting statistical matter bearing on the commercial aspects of instrument-making.

Of obsolete instruments, the lute has probably received the greatest attention. Vincentio Galilei's *Il Fronimo* (Venice, 1585 : folio), and Mace's *Musick's Monument* (London, 1676 : folio), in which much interesting information will be found, have both been already referred to. Probably the most recent, and certainly one of the most valuable, works on the instrument is E. G. Baron's *Historich Theoretisch und Practische Untersuchung*

des Instruments der Lauten (Nürnberg,
1727: 8vo), with portrait of the author
and several woodcuts, the title of which
sufficiently indicates its scope. The
musette, a species of small bagpipes,
which attained so great a vogue in France
during the reign of Louis XIV. was
treated of in a sumptuous work by C. E.
Borjon, an advocate of the Parlement of
Paris, and a voluminous writer on juris-
prudence. The work is entitled *Traité
de la Musette* (Lyons, 1672 : folio), and is
illustrated with admirable engravings.
It is of considerable rarity. Although
written in the first person singular the
author's name appears nowhere in the
work—not even in the privilege.

The number of patents which have
been granted for improvements in musical
instruments is enormous. The specification of any one of these is to be obtained
at the Patent Office, while excellent
abridgments of them have been published in three volumes, at a moderate
price, bringing the information down to
the end of 1883. The last volume, which
is on much larger paper, has the advantage
of being illustrated with diagrams.

We have omitted to mention the *Gabin-
etto Armonico* of P. Bonanni (Rome, 1723 :
4to), a book of plates of instruments,

with descriptions. Many of the instruments are imaginary, and the book is
absolutely valueless. A second edition,
with a French translation, was given by
the Abbé Cerutti in 1776.

CHAPTER XI.

THE LITERATURE OF MUSIC AS A SCIENCE.

THE investigation of the laws of sound has occupied much of the attention of men of science from an early time. The division of the monochord formed the subject of most of the Greek writers on Music, and in more modern times equally attracted the attention of Mersenne, Kircher, and Descartes, whose writings have already been referred to. Scarcely any mathematician of eminence can be named who, at some period of his career, has not treated of such questions as the vibrations of strings, the production of sound by musical pipes, or the relations of the intervals. Among these we may mention Wallis, Newton, Brooke Taylor, the Bernouillis (James I. and David), Euler, Diderot, and D'Alembert. These researches are generally contained in papers addressed to various academies and learned societies, in the transactions of which they must be sought for, unless the works of the author have been published in a collected form. To give any particulars here would be impossible.

Towards the end of the last century Chladni was led to investigate the phenomena of sound experimentally. His most valuable researches are probably those on the vibrations of plates, but the whole subject of acoustics is treated of in his *Akustik* (Leipzig, 1802 : 4to), a work which was translated into French under the title of *Traité d'acoustique* (Paris, 1809 : 8vo), at the instance of the Emperor Napoleon, who found the means. An excellent and appreciative account of Chladni's discoveries will be found in Professor Tyndall's *Sound*.

It is much to be regretted that the investigations of Savart into the principles involved in the construction of musical instruments are not available in a collected form. His toothed wheel was one of the earliest attempts at an absolute measure of pitch, but this was soon set aside by the invention of Cagniard de la Tour's " siren," which greatly facilitated the determination of absolute pitch. Few subjects have made more rapid advances in modern times than acoustics, mainly owing to the labours of the renowned physicist the late Professor Helmholtz, whose work, *Die Lehre von Tonempfind-ungen*, first published in 1863, is a complete encyclopædia of the subject, and should be in the hands of every one who takes an interest in the " scientific basis " of the art of Music. The work has been translated into English by Mr. A. J. Ellis, himself an authority on kindred subjects, who has added much valuable matter. Two editions of this translation have appeared: the last and most complete is London 1885, 8vo. It is impossible to give an analysis of so comprehensive and elaborate a work in the space at our disposal; probably the most important feature is that the different qualities of tone produced by different musical instruments (" *timbre* ") are for the first time explained as depending on the harmonics produced by the note sounded; and it is by the invention of his " resonators " that it has become possible to disengage and identify these harmonic sounds.

The first attempt at popularising the scientific principles of Music is to be found in Euler's *Lettres à une Princesse d'Alle-magne* (earliest edition, St. Petersburg, 1768-72: 3 vols., 8vo; but frequently reprinted). Of works embracing the discoveries of Helmholtz we may mention *Sound,* by the late Professor Tyndall (London, 1867 : 8vo ; with several reprints), which shows his marvellous skill in popularising scientific questions ; Mr. Sedley Taylor's *Sound and Music* (London, 1873 : 8vo) ; Mr. J. Broadhouse's *Student's Helmholtz* (London, 1881 : 8vo), a useful little book, well carrying out its title ; Dr. Pole's *'Philosophy of Music* (London, 1879 : 8vo) ; and the late Dr. W. H. Stone's happily named *Scientific Basis of Music,* one of Messrs. Novello's music primers, which gives much information in a small compass. In French an excellent little work is V. C. Mahillon's *Eléments d'Acoustique musicale et instrumentale* (Brussels, 1874 : 8vo). Blaserna's *Teoria del suono* (Florence, 1875 : 8vo) has been translated in the "International Scientific Series."

To follow the subject in its higher developments considerable mathematical knowledge is necessary. Those who are thus equipped will find the most recent knowledge in the work *On Sound and Atmospheric Vibrations* of the late Sir G. B. Airy (London, 1868 : 8vo ; there is a second edition), and in the *Theory of Sound,* by Lord Rayleigh (London, 1877 :

2 vols., 8vo) a second edition of which is also in the press.

The subject of tuning and temperament has a large literature of its own. It is generally stated that J. S. Bach was the first to advocate practically the use of equal temperament in his *Wohltemperirte Clavier,* and there is no doubt that this method of tuning received the support of the great theorists, such as Sorge, Kirnberger, and Marpurg ; but it was a long time before the mean-tone method of tuning was abandoned, in favour of equal temperament, even in Germany, while in this country it was first adopted at Messrs. Broadwood's in 1846, and for the organ in 1854. The practice has now become universal, and has been accepted by nearly every practical musician. Excellent books on the subject are Rev. John Curwen's *Tract on Musical Statics* (London, 1874 : square 8vo) and Mr. Bosanquet's *Elementary Treatise on Musical Intervals and Temperament* (London, 1876: 8vo), while the subject is treated with fuller detail in the work of Helmholtz.

During the prevalence of the mean-tone method many schemes were propounded for the distribution of the wolf, and for rendering the remoter keys available. Among the first of these was that contained in Dr. Robert Smith's *Harmonics*, the second edition of which (London, 1759 : 8vo) contains "a postscript upon the changeable harpsichord." This consisted in a mechanical method of modifying the tuning according to the key, and at least had the advantage of leaving the keyboard untouched. Maxwell, in his *Essay upon Tune*, published anonymously (Edinburgh, 1781 : 2 vols., 8vo), proposes an organ with several ranks of pipes for each stop, to be brought on to the key-board by different stop-knobs. The Rev. Henry Liston, of Ecclesmachan, in his *Essay on Perfect Intonation* (Edinburgh, 1812 : 4to), proposed to modify the pitch of the flue pipes by shades brought over the tops, and in the case of stopt pipes, over the mouth. Neither of these contrivances was, of course, applicable to reed stops.

Two other schemes have been advanced with great enthusiasm by their authors. The first is explained in *The Principles and Practice of Just Intonation . . . as illustrated in the Enharmonic Organ*, by General T. Perronet Thompson, F.R.S. This instrument contained forty sounds to the octave, requiring as many pipes, and could "perform correctly in twenty-one keys with their minors to the extent of involving not more than five flats." This required three rows of keys, each very complicated in construction, which rendered the use of the instrument exceedingly difficult. A blind girl, Miss E. L. Northcote, was, however, able to give a public performance on it after six lessons, and to her the later editions of the pamphlet, ten of which at least exist, are dedicated. General Thompson was a good mathematician, for a time Member for Hull, editor of the *Westminster Review*, and also well known for his energetic advocacy of the repeal of the Corn Laws. The pamphlet was freely distributed by the author.

Another scheme was propounded by an American, Mr. H. W. Poole, in a pamphlet which is much more difficult to meet with—*An Essay on Perfect Intonation; . . . together with a brief description of the Enharmonic Organ of Messrs. Alley & Poole* (Newhaven, 1850 : 8vo). Mr. Alley was an organ-builder of Newburyport, Mass., who put the plans of Mr. Poole into practical form. In the organ originally constructed the ordinary key-board was preserved, the necessary modifications in pitch being effected by means of pedals; but it was afterwards proposed to abandon this plan, in favour of a modification of the key-board. In the organ actually constructed the range of perfect keys was no greater than in that of General Thompson, and the tones were obtained in the same way, by increasing the number of pipes.

One more plan, in this case adapted to the harmonium, was propounded by Mr. Bosanquet, under the title of *The Generalised Fingerboard*, a description of which will be found in his work on temperament.

It will be noticed that none of these schemes originate with the practical musician, who in our own day is content to accept the method of equal temperament.

The practical application of equal temperament, involving careful estimation of the beats of tempered intervals, was not without difficulty. Much attention was given to the subject by H. Scheibler "Seidenwaaren-Manufacturist in Crefeld," as he always modestly describes himself on his title-pages. One of his inventions was the estimation of the number of beats by the oscillation of the metronome, and he also contrived a "Tonometer" of fifty-two tuning forks to the octave. His investigations will be found in *Der Physikalische und Musikalische Tonmesser*

(Essen, 1834 : 8vo), *Anleitung die Orgel vermittelst der Stösse (vulgo Schwebungen) und des Metronoms correct gleichschwebend zu stimmen* (Crefeld, 1834 : 8vo), and in a collected form, after his death, as *H. Scheibler's Schriften über musikalische und physikalische Tonmessung* (Crefeld, 1838 : 8vo). The mathematical relations of the intervals of the scale have been calculated by many men of science—in our own country by the late W. S. B. Woolhouse, in his *Essay on Musical Intervals* (London, 1835 : 8vo); while in France the late M. Delezenne was an industrious writer on the subject. For a list of his works we must refer the reader to Fétis.

The elegant experiments of Lissajous for rendering the vibrations of musical sounds, and their combinations, visible to the eye were originally published in the somewhat inaccessible form of a lecture delivered before the Société de compositeurs de Musique in 1863. A long extract from the paper will be found in the article "Lissajous" in the supplement to the *Dictionnaire* of Fétis. The various apparatus for these and other acoustical experiments are described in the excellent catalogues issued by Marloye and by Kœnig, both of Paris, as well as in *Die neueren Apparate der Akustik* of Prof. F. J. Pisko (Vienna, 1865 : 8vo).

The question of pitch is one which has been much discussed—not altogether without acrimony. The history of the subject has been exhaustively treated by the late Mr. A. J. Ellis in two papers read before the Society of Arts, March 5 and April 2, 1880, which were published in the Journal of the Society, and privately printed in a separate form. Mr. Ellis treats of the question again in the appendix to his last edition of Helmholtz. The number of pitches he has catalogued is wonderful.

There remains only to mention methods of measuring time in music. The first suggestion of the pendulum for that purpose is to be found in Loulié's *Elements ou Principes de la Musique* (Paris, 1696 : 8vo ; reprinted, Amsterdam, 1698 : 8vo). He calls his instrument a " Chronomètre." There was no contrivance for keeping the pendulum in motion, and the speed was expressed in terms of the length of the pendulum—a plan used early in this century in Germany, and in this country by Dr. Crotch. Such contrivances are, of course, superseded by the metronome, introduced, if not invented, by Maelzel.

CHAPTER XII.

The Bibliography of Music.

L T H O U G H c o m i n g under Charles Lamb's description of " books which are no books," there are few more useful works in the musical library than thematic catalogues of the compositions of the great musicians. The writer still retains a lively recollection of the delight afforded him, more than thirty-five years ago, by the acquisition of such a catalogue of Beethoven's works, which formed the first volume of a collection now very considerable.

As far as the writer knows, the first work of this nature published was the *Catalogo delle Sinfonie . . . in manuscritto* (and works of other natures), in the possession of J. G. Breitkopf, the founder of the famous and still flourishing house of Breitkopf & Härtel. It was begun in 1762, and completed with sixteen supplements, bringing it down to 1767.

It forms a wonderful guide to the music issued between these dates—perhaps not a very interesting period, but very valuable for the history of the art. It is not common, and fetches a good price when a copy offers. The writer's was formerly in the possession of John Bland, the music publisher, who was concerned in Salomon's negotiations with Haydn, and he seems to have followed Breitkopf's example by issuing a thematic catalogue of his own publications—probably the first *English* instance of the practice.

The earliest catalogue of the works of a particular composer is the well-known one of the works of Mozart, from February 9th, 1784, to November 15th, 1791, the original of which was carefully drawn up by his own hand. It was printed by J. André at Offenbach, in 1805, and subsequently more than once re-issued. But the most admirable of all catalogues is that of Mozart, by Ludwig von Köchel, (Leipzig, 1862 : large 8vo). It forms a worthy monument to the genius of the composer, and is full of the most interesting information.

The excellent catalogue of Beethoven's works was drawn up by Nottebohm (Leipzig, 1851 : large 8vo), although his name does not appear till the second edition (1868). This follows the order of the opus numbers, which, it is well known, in many cases do not agree with the chronological order of their composition. Mr. A. W. Thayer, an American, who has made the study of everything concerning Beethoven the work of his life, issued a *Chronologisches Verzeichniss*, (Berlin, 1865 : 8vo), in which the order of production is followed. On that account alone the work would be interesting, but the value is greatly enhanced by the additional information given.

Of Mendelssohn, Schubert, Schumann, Chopin, Liszt, excellent thematic catalogues are published. Messrs. Peters & Co. issue one of J. Sebastian Bach in two volumes (Leipzig, 1882 : 8vo), the first devoted to the instrumental, the other to the vocal works of the master. F. W. Jähn's *Carl Maria von Weber in seinen Werken* (Berlin, 1871 : large 8vo) is worthy to rank with Von Köchel's *Mozart* for its exhaustive treatment of the subject. It contains some good facsimiles of Weber's writing.

It is curious that no printed thematic catalogue exists of the works of Haydn. The fact that he himself drew up such a catalogue is well known, and a few manuscript copies of it are in existence—

one being in the writer's library—but it has never been printed, and now we fear the interest in his works is dying out. There is a thematic catalogue of his quartets published by Trautwein (Berlin, 1844 : 8vo).

Of non-thematic catalogues we have one of the works of Joachim Raff, by Albert Schäfer (Wiesbaden [1888] : 8vo), and an excellent catalogue of the works of Rubinstein was brought out on the occasion of his jubilee (Leipzig, [1890] : 4to).

It must be admitted that for nearly all our musical bibliographies we are indebted to the industry and painstaking accuracy of Germans. To his translation of Delmotte's *Roland de Lattre* (Berlin, 1837 : 8vo), S. W. Dehn added a careful catalogue of that composer's works. This has been partly superseded by the more modern information contained in that compiled by R. Eitner, and originally brought out as a supplement to the *Monatshefte für Musikgeschichte*, an excellent publication, which has also contained catalogues of the compositions of Hans Leo Hassler, J. B. Hasse, as well as of the musical works contained in the libraries of Augsburg, the Joachimsthal Gymnasium in Berlin, the University

Library at Göttingen, and the Ritter-Akademie at Liegnitz. Here also appeared the very useful *Verzeichniss neuer Ausgabe alter Musik werke*, by Robert Eitner, of the greatest value to those who are seeking for available means of becoming acquainted with the rich legacy of old times. This, and some of the other catalogues, have been separately published.

An excellent attempt at a complete catalogue of music printed during the sixteenth and seventeenth centuries, arranged chronologically in classes, was made by C. F. Becker (Leipzig, 2nd edition, 1855 : 4to), which will be found very useful. There is also an admirable bibliography of *collections—i.e.*, publications comprising works by more than one composer—drawn up by Haberl, Lagerberg, and Pohl, under the editorship of R. Eitner, entitled *Bibliographie der Musik-sammel-werke der XVI. und XVII. Jahrhunderts*, provided with excellent indexes (Berlin, 1877 : 8vo). The equally valuable *Bibliothek der Gedruckten Weltlichen Vocal Musik Italiens* 1500—1700, by Dr. Emil Vogel (Berlin, 1892 : 2 vols., 8vo), arranged under the names of the composers, was published at the charges of the "Stiftung von Schnyder von Wartersee," with preface, etc., both in

German and Italian. These works are absolutely necessary to any one studying the music of this period. It would be a boon if a similar catalogue of sacred music were undertaken by the same competent hands.

In the English language, the only works of this nature we can refer to are the late Dr. Rimbault's *Bibliotheca Madrigaliana* (London : 8vo) a well-executed work, and a catalogue of a collection of song-books formed by Sir John Stainer ; but this, we believe, is privately printed.

Of catalogues of public libraries of musical works perhaps the most important is that of the Liceo Musicale of Bologna, originally made by Gaetano Gaspari, but edited and published, after his death, by F. Parisini and L. Torchi, under the auspices of the Municipio of that city. It is contained in three handsome volumes (Bologna, 1890–93 : 8vo), devoted severally to theory, history, etc., to sacred music, and to secular music. It is an excellent catalogue of an admirable library, and enriched with notes full of information. The noble library formed by Fétis, now the property of Belgium, has been well catalogued (Paris, 1877 : 8vo). Herr Peters, the well-known music-publisher of Leipzig, has presented that city with a well-selected library for the special advantage of the large number of students resorting to that place, of which a good catalogue has been printed (Leipzig, 1894 : 8vo). The printed music of the Stadtbibliothek and other libraries of Breslau has been catalogued up to the year 1700 by E. Bohn (Breslau, 1883 : 8vo), and the manuscripts in the former library by the same capable hands (*ib.*, 1890 : 8vo).

An admirable library of music was collected by John IV., King of Portugal (1604—1656). The fact was known, but the library had entirely disappeared, and a conjecture was made that it was lost in the earthquake at Lisbon. Fortunately a copy of the first part of the catalogue was discovered in the National Library at Paris, and this has been reprinted in a noble quarto volume (Lisbon, 1874), under the superintendence of Señor J. de Vasconcellos, who has also published an essay on the treasures which this collection contained (Oporto, 1873 : 4to).

M. Weckerlin, the esteemed librarian of the Conservatoire of Paris, has issued a *Catalogue bibliographique* of the rarer works in that library, both theoretical and practical (Paris, 1885 : 8vo). It forms an interesting volume, and is illustrated with facsimiles, etc.

We are indebted to Dom F. X. Haberl for an excellent catalogue of the priceless contents of the library of the papal chapel in the Vatican, entitled, *Bibliographischer und Thematischer Musikkatalog des Papstlichen Kapellarchives*, etc. (Leipzig, 1888 : 8vo). This appeared originally in the *Monatshefte*, and until its publication no certain information existed as to the contents of this collection, owing to the jealousy with which these treasures were guarded.

This does not exhaust the printed catalogues of foreign libraries, but we have no space to give further titles. In England the late Mr. T. Oliphant drew up *A Catalogue of the Manuscript Music in the British Museum*, printed by order of the trustees in 1842 (8vo), good up to that date, but of course now much behindhand. The proposal to print a catalogue of all the music in that Institution down to 1800, which would be a real boon to students, appears to be in abeyance. It seems a great waste of exceptional acquirements that the time of the accomplished gentlemen who preside over that Department should be mainly occupied in cataloguing the last set of waltzes, or the vulgar inanities of the Music-hall,—no doubt a sad necessity, but surely a task within the powers of an intelligent lad. The municipal authorities of a comparatively small Italian city can find the funds to compile and print an admirable catalogue of the musical treasures committed to their charge, while the National Library of the richest nation in the world is, for lack of means, unable to follow so excellent an example !

The library of the late Sacred Harmonic Society, under the fostering care of its excellent honorary librarian, the late Mr. W. H. Husk, grew to be one of great importance, especially as to English madrigals, in which it must be unapproached. Several editions of the catalogue were issued, the last in 1872 (8vo), a monument of Mr. Husk's painstaking care. A supplement was published in 1882. The collection has now passed into the possession of the Royal College of Music. A valuable musical library was bequeathed, by the late Mr. William Euing, of Glasgow, to Anderson's Library, for the production of a catalogue of which he left a sum of £200. The work was unfortunately entrusted to wholly incompetent hands, and, moreover, by the terms of the will no copy could be sold.

It is a pity that a really valuable collection should be thus rendered almost useless. We must finally mention the catalogue of the music in the Fitzwilliam Museum Library at Cambridge, a collection which contains the famous *Queen Elizabeth's Virginal Book*, and is also very rich in Handel manuscripts. The catalogue was made by Mr. J. A. Fuller-Maitland and Dr. Mann, the latter of whom undertook the Handel collection with great success.

Passing over the scattered notices of works on Music, such as those contained in the well-known *Polyhistor* of Morhof, the first attempt at a separate bibliography of the subject appears to be that made by Gruber, under the titles *Litteratur der Musik* (Nuremberg, 1783–5 : 2 vols., 8vo) and *Beyträge zur Litteratur der Musik* (Frankfort, 1790 : 2 vols., 8vo), both which works are absolutely identical, the title only having been changed. The work is of small value. A much better attempt was made by J. G. Forkel in his *Allgemeine Litteratur der Musik* (Leipzig, 1792 : 8vo), a volume of five hundred and forty pages, consisting of a *catalogue raisonnée* of musical literature. This work forms the basis of two other praiseworthy attempts, the first of which was the *Bibliografia della Musica* of Dr. P. Lichtenthal, issued in conjunction with his dictionary (Milan, 1826 : 4 vols., 8vo). This was succeeded by C. F. Becker's *Systematisch-chronologische Darstellung der Musikalischen Litteratur* (Leipzig, 1836 : 4to), brought down by a supplement to 1839. A further supplement by R. Eitner is to be found in the *Monatshefte*, which the writer thinks has not been issued separately, so that it is not very available. Mr. Andrew Deakin, of Birmingham, has compiled an excellent bibliography of works on Music, published in England, arranged chronologically (Birmingham, 1892 : 4to). He is now engaged on a revised edition, in which he proposes to include all musical compositions of any importance brought out in this country down to the year 1800—a vast undertaking, the value of which cannot be over-estimated. The *Bibliographie Musicale* of César Gardeton, published anonymously (Paris, 1822 : 8vo), is futile and useless.

The *Récherches historiques concernant les Journaux de Musique* of E. G. J. Gregoir (Antwerp, 1872 : 8vo) will be found a useful catalogue of such publications, giving the date of first publication, and of their extinction, when this has arrived. W. Freystätter's *Die Musik-alischer Zeitschriften* (Munich, 1884 : 8vo) is avowedly based on the earlier work, and is somewhat more detailed.

Several interesting loan collections of musical works have been made. The first of these was in connexion with the Caxton Exhibition in 1877. The whole collection was admirably catalogued—the musical department by Messrs. Littleton, Cummings, and Barrett. This catalogue was as excellent as the next was disgrace-ful—that of the Loan Exhibition in the Albert Hall during the Inventions Exhibition of 1885, which was a mere hand list, of the most meagre description. At the instance of Mr. Quaritch, Mr. W. H. J. Weale was induced to compile a *Descriptive Catalogue of Rare Manuscripts and Printed Books, chiefly liturgical* (London, 1886 : 8vo), so that some, at least, of the very rare works exhibited were adequately described.

There are other more modest sources of information, which must not be over-looked by the ardent bibliographer. Such, for example, are auction catalogues of a past day, among the most interesting of which are those of the libraries of Rev. William Gostling, Minor Canon of Canter-bury, and son of Purcell's friend, dispersed so long ago as 1777; of James Bartleman in 1822; and in more modern days those of the late Professor E. Taylor, and of the Libri sale;—not to speak of those which have taken place in foreign countries. Nor must the trade catalogues of dealers in old music and its literature be neglected, especially when drawn up with such exceptional knowledge as that possessed by Mr. L. Liepmannssohn, of Berlin, to whom the writer is glad to acknowledge his great indebtedness.

We must now bring these remarks to a close, although the subject is very far from exhausted. Our own pursuits have taught us the increased zest which is given to our musical enjoyments by some acquaintance with the history of the Art, with the aims of those who have followed it, and with the development of cultivated opinion on their productions. To introduce the reader to the best sources of information on these subjects has been the object of this book. A work of this nature is, of necessity, imperfect, and no doubt many interesting branches of musical knowledge will be found untouched, many valuable treatises unmentioned. In the space at our disposal it has only been possible to mention those works which are of the most general interest, or of the greatest utility ; but we trust that the information we have been able to give may start many on a voyage of discovery which will prove both pleasant and profitable.

INDEX.